Just Follow Jesus

Jordan Richardson

JUST FOLLOW JESUS by Jordan Richardson

First Edition

Published by By Faith Publishing

Copyright © 2025 Jordan Richardson

Author Services by Pedernales Publishing, LLC.
www.pedernalespublishing.com

Library of Congress Control Number: 2025919371

ISBN: 979-8-9995309-2-9 Paperback Edition
        979-8-9995309-1-2 Hardcover Edition
        979-8-9995309-0-5 Digital Edition

Printed in the United States of America

Dedicated to my incredible family.

Traci, Mason, Granny, Gramps, Joshua,
I couldn't have done any of this without you.

Love you always!!

Just Follow Jesus

INTRODUCTION

When the idea to write a devotional book first came to me, I immediately knew what its title would be: *Just Follow Jesus*. I chose this title for a few reasons. First, <u>following Jesus</u> is what this entire book is about. Every page you're about to read centers around who Jesus is and how we can choose to follow Him in our daily lives, no matter what we're going through. This is a simple yet profound and all-encompassing statement that we must keep in our minds as we face every circumstance. In fact, my beloved grandmother (Granny) and I used to say it on the phone to each other at the end of every conversation, just to remind ourselves.

But there's more to my choice than just that. These words mean something special to my family and me. *Just Follow Jesus* was the last thing my father said to five-month-old me before I went into the operating room to receive a double-lung transplant.

I was born with an incredibly rare genetic disease that kept my lungs from working. It's normally fatal, but by the hand of God alone, I survived long enough for the transplant. I won't get into all the details of my story, but there are a few things you need to understand so you will fully grasp my message more as we work through this book.

First, transplant life is tricky. There's no way to sugarcoat that. Some think that the medical difficulties end once the actual transplant surgery is over. While I do want to be very clear that I am unspeakably grateful for the transplant, which literally did save my life, I also want to be clear that the challenges don't end at that point. A new set of challenges begins.

You've no doubt heard about the "immunocompromised" or "vulnerable" population who have very low immune systems (especially on the news during COVID). Well, that's me. I've been a part of this population all my life and always will be. And that's hard.

It means avoiding close contact with large groups and people I don't know at all costs because I can't risk getting sick with anything, from the simplest cold to COVID. It means constantly worrying about random diseases and infections that a normal person wouldn't even notice. Add that to the constant concern that things could go super wrong at any point and … yeah, it can have its struggles.

But this book isn't just about the hard moments. Yes, I'll share some of that along the way. However, this book is more about how God shows up in each and every one of those bad times and hard moments—mine and yours too.

God has shown me so much throughout my life. A few years ago, I started sharing my story and my God-moments via inspirational videos on YouTube. As more and more people shared how they were encouraged by these videos, I continued recording new ones. I now have over two-hundred! Now I feel like God is calling me to share them in a new way: this book.

I think it's important to always be intentional and to have a purpose behind what I do. Here's what I wrote down as mine when I first began this book:

To bring awareness to transplant life, but even more than that, bring awareness to the God that's been with me longer than the transplant has.

To encourage people that no matter what they're going through, they must never give up—because you never know what God's going to do with your story."

An incredible friend once said that I could see the things I've been through as a pain or as a platform. I want mine to be a platform to spread God's Word and His hope to everyone that I can. That's what ultimately drives me to share my story with you.

I don't want to portray myself as doing each of these things perfectly. I fail and fall down all the time. I hurt, struggle, and worry more than I should. But I want us all to see those challenges as lessons God has taught me through my various experiences because that way, we can work on them together.

Each of these devotionals is a new way that I have learned to *Just Follow Jesus* throughout my life as I've faced different struggles. I am praying that each one will encourage you, uplift you, and more than that, draw you closer to God and help you *Just Follow Jesus* in new ways in your life.

Thank you so much for stepping into this book with me. I can't wait to take this journey with you!

WHO DO YOU FOLLOW?

Matthew 16:24 - "Then Jesus said to His disciples, 'If anyone desires to come after Me, let him deny himself, and take up his cross, and follow Me.'" (NKJV)

I wanted this to be the very first devotional you'll read for a reason. Not only does it tie into the title of this book, but it's the message I want this entire book to boil down to.

Whether we realize it or not, we all ultimately choose to follow something. This choice guides all our decisions, shapes the way we view the world, and forms the very person we are. What is that for you?

The world has an answer to that question: "Follow your heart!" If you've ever seen a Hallmark movie or an animated Barbie movie, you're familiar with this phrase. It's basically the entire message of all those movies. Don't misunderstand me—I love Hallmark movies, and I think I have almost every animated Barbie movie on DVD (and I can probably sing all of the songs too). But their use of that message always made me pause.

6

I'm willing to bet you know this idea without ever seeing those movies, though. It's all around our culture. It's the idea of putting yourself first and that listening to your own heart, pursuing your own desires above all else, and doing what feels right to you is the only way to find happiness.

As Christians, though, we believe something different. The Bible talks about what it's really like to follow our hearts. Jeremiah 17:9 calls the heart "deceitful above all things" and "desperately wicked."

Wow—talk about some strong wording, right? Do you want something "wicked" and full of lies to be your guide? I certainly don't.

So, what's the alternative? As Christians, our question turns from "What do you follow?" to "WHO do you follow?"

We choose to follow Jesus. Not our "deceitful and wicked" hearts. Not our own judgments. *Jesus.*

It's not easy. It goes against what the world and culture will tell us to do. But I can guarantee you, there is no better choice than the choice to *just follow Jesus.*

Personal Reflection: What, or who, do you currently follow? Does that need to change?

_____

_____

_____

_____

_____

_____

_____

_____

_____

_____

_____

_____

_____

_____

_____

WEEK 2

BE STILL

Psalm 46:10 - "Be still and know that I am God ..."
(NKJV)

Have you ever noticed just how *hard* it is to be still?
You probably have, but on the off-chance you haven't
noticed, try it right now. Put this book down and try to
be still for just twenty seconds. Sit quietly, without doing
anything. I'll wait.

Done? Okay. How'd it go? I can tell you how it would go
for me—my mind would start to wander to all the things
I need to do or the people I want to reach out to or what
I'm having for dinner, etc. The truth is, even when my body
may be outwardly still, my mind certainly isn't. Being still
is uncomfortable for me, and I'm guessing it is for you too.

Humans don't instinctively want to be still, especially not
when bad things are happening. We want to fix it all.

Yet God calls us to *be still*.

The good news is that's not all there is to the verse. God

knows how hard it is for us, so he adds specific instructions: *… and know that I am God.*

What does that mean? We're not just *still* for no reason. We're not *still* in the sense that we sit down, throw our hands in the air, and give up. We're *still* because we are taking time to focus on who God is. We're *still* because we're at peace; we're at peace because we *know* who God is.

Now, try the twenty-second exercise again, but this time think of an attribute of God, a Bible verse that means a lot to you (Psalm 46:10, perhaps?), or maybe a Christian song.

How'd it go this time? No matter what is going on in your life, hear this call from God today: *Be still and know that I am God.*

I wrote this poem during a time when my own mind was racing with different troubles and cares. In the midst of this struggle, God clearly showed me that He wanted me to just *be still*, no matter what, because He had a plan.

The ground beneath is shaking
My heart's at risk of breaking
Yet You ask me to Be Still.
I see the skies turning gray
And ask "Will I be okay?"
You just say to Be Still.
My fear stops me in my tracks
I look to You for the facts
You calmly say Be Still.
I think of ways I should brace
My mind continues to race

11

You ask me to Be Still.
You reach down and take my hand
And though I don't understand
You teach me to Be Still.
Though I don't know what to do
I know that I can trust in You
And I promise to Be Still.

Personal Reflection: Take time to be still in the Lord's presence this week. Write about how the time went.

_____

_____

_____

_____

_____

_____

_____

_____

_____

_____

_____

_____

_____

WEEK 3

GOD KNOWS YOU

Nahum 1:7 – "The Lord is good, a stronghold in the day of trouble, and He knows those who take refuge in Him." (NASB)

Have you ever felt like no one understood what you were going through? I can tell you, I know that feeling. As someone who has received a double-lung transplant, the best word to sum up my life would probably be "complicated." (In fact, now that I think about it, my mom uses that word all the time to describe me!)

There are so many aspects of transplant life that are nearly impossible to explain. I very much appreciate friends who ask me questions and genuinely want to know more about it, but I know they can never fully understand, just as I know I can never fully understand everything they've been through. None of us knows every detail of what another person has been through or is walking through right now, even if we think we do.

I sometimes wonder what people must think as they watch

how I live, and I think to myself, *if they only knew.* If they only knew all the different things my family and I've gone through. If they only knew the risks. If they only knew how hard it is. If they only knew …

Do you relate?

That's why Nahum 1:7 is one of my favorite verses. God calls us to take *refuge* in Him. The official definition of refuge is "shelter or protection from danger, trouble, etc.."[1] Whatever trouble you are facing, God wants to be your refuge. He wants you to feel safe in the shelter of His love!

This also comes with a promise: God *knows* us! He knows every detail of our lives. He knows the hard things we've been through. He knows our hearts. He knows how many hairs are on our head (and, for me, yikes, is that a lot!). He knows how you're feeling in the middle of the night when no one is around. He knows every thought.

God knows you and loves you. Find comfort in that amazing love, and find safety in the shelter that He offers.

---

1. *Dictionary.com,* s.v. "refuge," accessed July 27, 2025, https://www.dictionary.com/browse/refuge

Personal Reflection: Think about one thing that no one knows about you (you don't have to write it down; just think about it). What does it mean to you that God knows about it, and that He still loves you?

_____

_____

_____

_____

_____

_____

_____

_____

_____

_____

_____

_____

_____

_____

WEEK 4

GOD NEVER CHANGES

Malachi 3:6 – "For I am the Lord, I do not change ..."
(NKJV)

In this world, there are very few things that can be described as God describes Himself in the verse above: unchanging. In fact, I challenge you to think of anything other than God that doesn't change. Can't think of anything? Me neither!

Change is such a constant part of life. Summer turns to fall, day turns to night, and people come and go from our lives. Big changes and small changes, good changes and bad changes—they always surround us. Maybe you're in a season where you feel like everything in your life is changing all at once.

In a world where everything is changing, and we have no control over what will change next or how, this verse is so reassuring. *God never changes.* Hebrews 13:8 echoes this same idea: "Jesus Christ is the same yesterday, today, and forever." (NKJV)

God's love never changes. God's faithfulness never changes. God's nearness never changes. God is the one and only constant that you can always rely on, no matter what is going on in your life. And you can rest in knowing that He controls everything. All the changes going on around you are orchestrated by Him.

It should give us incredible peace that, in the midst of chaotic and unpredictable circumstances, the unchanging God is the one who is in charge of it all.

Because of my transplant, I never know when my life is going to change. I've had ups and downs with my health and with my life that I never saw coming. I bet you have too. But knowing that God never changes, even when my life does, gives me peace no matter what current circumstances I find myself in.

Take hold of this promise today:

Has everything in your life changed? He hasn't.

Has the world around you changed? He hasn't.

Have you changed? He hasn't.

Personal Reflection: What is the biggest change you've ever gone through? How does it help you to know that through each change and through each day, God stays the same?

_____

_____

_____

_____

_____

_____

_____

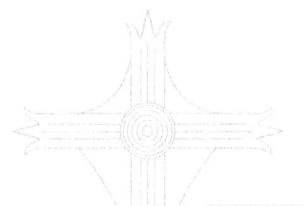

BE STRONG AND COURAGEOUS

Joshua 1:9 - "Have I not commanded you? Be strong and courageous. Do not be afraid; do not be discouraged, for the Lord your God will be with you wherever you go." (NIV)

I'm excited about this devotional because I get to write about my absolute, all-time favorite Bible verse. (Clearly, I couldn't wait very long to do it!) This verse has been my favorite for many years; I even bought a necklace a few years ago, during a really rough time, that has this verse written on the back of it. That necklace has gone with me to countless doctors' appointments and hospital trips. I've worn it on days when I had a big school test I was worried about or on days when I simply felt like I needed the reminder.

One reason Joshua 1:9 is my favorite is that each part of it is so meaningful. First off, God reminds us that this is a *command* from Him. This part of the verse is often cut out when I see it referenced outside of the Bible (for example, it's not written on my necklace), but I don't want us to overlook it.

When your leader, your director, or any authority figure over you gives you a direct command, shouldn't you obey it? That's what is happening here: the words that follow come not as a suggestion or something we should do when we feel like it, but as a command from our Leader and Savior. If we obey our earthly authority figures, shouldn't we want to obey a command given to us by God?

So, what's the command? To *be strong and courageous, not afraid or discouraged.* Wow, is that hard! I have enough trouble with this on a regular day when nothing is going on, but try doing it when you've lost your job. When your family is coming apart. When (as in my case) you're at the doctor's office waiting to hear what your test results show. How are we supposed to obey such a tough command in such a scary, discouraging, painful world?

The good news is this: God doesn't leave us in that place with nothing. He doesn't give us this command and walk away. He knows how hard this is, so He gives us a reason why this command can and should be obeyed: *He is with us wherever we go.*

The fact that God is always with us, no matter what we face, should bring us all the comfort and assurance we need to act out this verse in every situation of our lives. Be strong. Be courageous. God is with you always.

Personal Reflection: What areas of your life are you struggling to be "strong and courageous" in today? What areas have you discouraged? What would change about them if you remembered Joshua 1:9?

_____

_____

_____

_____

_____

_____

_____

_____

_____

_____

_____

_____

_____

_____

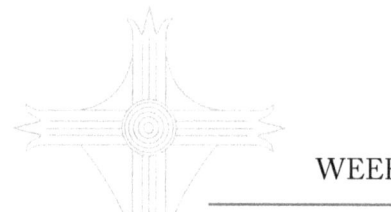

WEEK 6

GIVE GOD YOUR WEIGHT

1 Peter 5:7 - "Cast all your anxiety on Him because He cares for you." (NIV)

Do you ever feel like you are struggling with so much that it weighs you down? Are there times when it is all just too hard to carry?

I want you to try something with me (or, if you can't, then just envision it). Grab a large bag (make sure it has large straps on it). Now, grab things that represent what you are struggling with the most—what's weighing you down.

For instance, when I did this exercise, I filled my bag with empty medicine bottles, N-95 hospital-grade masks, and other things to represent my health struggles. I also filled it with the new syllabus for the college class I had just started. Fill yours with tokens that represent your deepest worries and pains. If you can't find anything to represent it, write it down on a piece of paper and throw that in the bag.

Now put the bag on! If your straps are large enough, put

it around your neck. Then try to walk around. This demonstrates how we go through each of our days—wearing this weight tied around our necks. Uncomfortable. Painful. Dragging us down. Limiting us.

We often don't even recognize that we're doing this, but what's the first thing you think of when you wake up? Is it all your troubles? If so, you are immediately putting this bag of weight around your neck before you even get out of bed.

So, what do we do? Thankfully, God doesn't want us to carry these burdens! He doesn't want us held down by all the things in our lives that we struggle with. That's what this verse above reminds us of.

If you still have your bag, take it off now (you're welcome!). Now imagine that you are laying it at the feet of Jesus, handing it off to Him. Say a prayer asking Him to take all these things from you. He wants to do it. He stands watching, feeling our pain, and hoping that we will give it all over to Him. Hebrews 4:16 reminds us we can come "boldly" to God's throne, where we will find "mercy and find grace to help in time of need" (NKJV).

When you love someone, you don't want to see them hurting and carrying their burdens alone. You want to carry it all for them. That's the love of God. He asks us to give all our cares and anxieties to Him *because He cares for us!* Every time you start to feel like you're weighed down and burdened, give all those struggles over to God. He loves you, and He wants to carry them for you.

Personal Reflection: Try this out! Write down what you put into your bag. How did it feel when it was all hanging on you? Try laying it all at Jesus's feet throughout this week. Then write about what it felt like.

_____

_____

_____

_____

_____

_____

_____

_____

_____

_____

_____

_____

_____

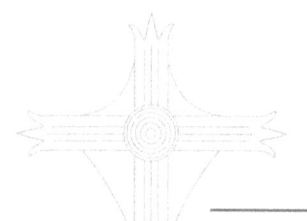

WEEK 7

LIGHT OF THE WORLD

Matthew 5:14, 16 – "You are the light of the world ...
Let your light so shine before men, that they may see
your good works and glorify your Father in heaven."
(NKJV)

Let's face it: our world is in darkness. This is a different kind of darkness than what comes just when the sun goes down. I'm talking about the darkness that's constant, that we feel and have inside us, whether it's the middle of the night or the middle of the day.

There are different reasons people feel this kind of darkness: depression, loneliness, sadness, grief, etc. But, I believe the biggest and worst kind of darkness is the darkness of those who don't know Christ. They don't even know how much darkness they are in. But it's very real.

God calls each of us to be the *light of the world*. It's important to realize why He calls us this. It's not because we are able to create light on our own, but because we have God's light in us. 1 John 1:5 clearly tells us that *God* is the source of all light, and God has put His light into each of His followers. Every time we feel like we have no light left, we need to remember where the light comes from.

Jesus goes on to tell us that the incredible gift of His light comes with a calling: to *let our light shine* to everyone around us so that God can be glorified through it. This makes me think of my mom because it's something she always says to do (and does better than anyone I know): reflect God's glory.

What does that look like? It means sharing God's love and His character with those around us. This will look different for each of us considering the gifts God has given us, the places He's put us in, and the relationships He ordains for us. Whether this means sharing the Gospel with friends, reaching out to someone in need, or sitting with a friend who is hurting, this is something we all can and should do every day.

Let God guide you and show you the details of where and how He wants you to shine your light. I know it may feel like your little light won't do much good in this vast darkness we live in. But take heart when God tells you, "The light shines in the darkness, and the darkness has not overcome it" (John 1:5, NIV).

Your light matters. Your light makes a difference. God has given you this light and placed you in these circumstances for a reason. Go out and shine your light into the dark world today, reflecting God's glory.

Personal Reflection: Write down three ways you can shine your light into the darkness this week ... then go do them! Write about each experience.

_____

_____

_____

_____

_____

_____

_____

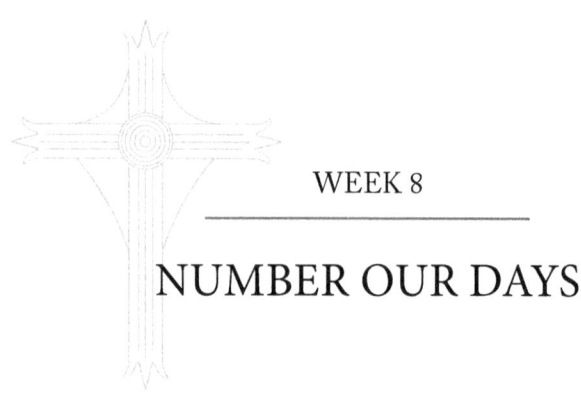

NUMBER OUR DAYS

Psalm 90:12 – "So teach us to number our days, that we may gain a heart of wisdom." (NKJV)

I'll be honest with you ... I never used to like this verse. I always struggled with the idea that I had to number my days. First off, I just hate numbers in general (I'm terrible at math!), but I also hate the reminder that tomorrow is not guaranteed.

Maybe you can relate to this. If so, hang in there because it is an important lesson for all of us.

We see right away that the verse begins with the words *teach us*. That should confirm that using our time wisely is not natural for us as humans. It's something we must learn to do and practice. If we did it automatically, we wouldn't need to be taught!

To number our days—what does that mean? Should we literally count up all the days we've been alive—1, 2, 300, 4,000, etc.? No, of course not! Does it mean that we need to live in constant fear that today might be the last day? That's what I used to think this verse meant, and sometimes I still slip into thinking that. But no. That's not it, either.

What's being said is that we need to be *mindful* of the fact that each day is a gift. No day is guaranteed. No one can promise that even if you do all the right things, you will live a long life. But I'll say it again for people out there like me—God does not want us to be afraid of how finite life is. He wants us to be aware so we will thank Him for each day He graciously gives us and choose to make the most out of it.

If we begin to do this, we begin pursuing, as the verse tells us, a *heart of wisdom*.

Personal Reflection: How would your life change if you lived in a way where you considered each day as a gift?

_____

_____

_____

_____

_____

_____

_____

WEEK 9

_____

SURPRISE

Psalm 139:16 - "... all the days ordained for me were written in Your book before one of them came to be." (NIV)

What's the biggest surprise you've ever gotten? Surprises can come in many forms. Good surprises like birthday parties or special gifts can be amazing.

But there are also bad surprises. Some of them are small, like a big rainstorm coming when the weather forecast calls for a five percent chance of rain all day. (This just happened to me yesterday—while my family and I were on a walk!) Surprises like that perhaps bring an inconvenience or a passing frustration ... but what about bigger ones?

What about when you're told you've lost your job, or that your health is suddenly uncertain? When a loved one dies unexpectedly? What about surprises that completely rock our world and change everything?

I remember getting the surprise a few years ago that my

health had gotten much worse. It happened out of the blue, with no warning. Suddenly, I was looking at an entirely different reality, searching for solid ground in the midst of the shock.

These situations are when this verse should give us comfort. It's basically saying that *nothing takes God by surprise.* Nothing! God knows exactly what is going to happen in our lives, from the good surprises to the tiny, inconvenient surprises, to the earth-shattering surprises that we face. Yet not one of them is a surprise to God.

When I think of this truth, I imagine myself freaking out, frazzled, and panicked by what is going on. I'm trying to control it, or stop it, or just survive it. Then, I picture myself looking over to God, and seeing Him perfectly calm and peaceful. Why? Because He knew this was coming. It didn't surprise or shock or scare Him.

I picture Him comforting me or even giving me an assuring smile, because even though He knows I am scared and upset, He also knows that this "surprise" is all part of His plan (Rom. 8:28). He already knows what we will face each day, and He's orchestrated all of it to fit into His perfect plan for us.

So, the next time you are surprised and shaken by something in your life, look to God and know that He is calmly comforting you through it—because nothing takes Him by surprise.

Personal Reflection: What's the best surprise you've ever gotten? The worst? Read over this description of picturing God's calming presence in the midst of your fear and really try to imagine it. Write about what it makes you think or feel.

_____

_____

_____

_____

_____

_____

_____

_____

_____

_____

_____

_____

_____

_____

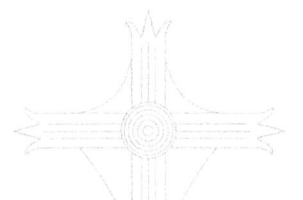

PONDERING VS. PARALYZED

Luke 2:19 - "But Mary treasured up all these things and pondered them in her heart." (NIV)

Have you ever noticed the importance of words? This is something my mom thinks about often, and she's shared these ideas with me. There is such significance in the words that we say, think, strive for, and use to describe ourselves.

Words are important to God, so therefore, they should be to us too. So, throughout this book, there will be some devotionals where I take two words and compare and contrast them. Here's our first one.

When you're faced with a struggle or fear, how do you handle it? For me, distraction equals trust. In other words, I have to take myself out of the situation to stop worrying about it. I have to get on my phone or watch something on YouTube or listen to music—anything that takes my mind off my troubles. That's how I trust God: I let Him handle it and I push it out of my mind. Maybe that's something you've done too.

But what if we can't distract ourselves? What if the struggle is in our face so much that there is literally no escaping it?

One night, I was paralyzed by the fears I was wrestling with. I couldn't sleep because of things that were going on in my life and thoughts I couldn't shut out of my mind. So, at three a.m., my mom and I talked about what to do when there is no escaping the fear.

Have you had nights like that? Those situations illustrate how important it is for us to be aware of what we *ponder*.

The official definition of *pondering* is "to consider something deeply and thoroughly"[2]

Contrast this meaning with the word *paralyzed,* which means "to bring to a condition of helpless stoppage, inactivity, or inability to act."[3]

When you face unescapable struggles, which path do you choose? I tend to be paralyzed. When I get into a situation that I can't distract myself from, I get so afraid that I can't think straight, move, or see clearly.

But notice that the definition of ponder has no mention of the word "fear." It's the idea of still moving forward, even in the midst of a bad and scary situation. It suggests that

2. *Dictionary.com,* s.v. "ponder," accessed July 27, 2025, https://www.dictionary.com/browse/ponder

3. *Dictionary.com,* s.v. "paralyze," accessed July 27, 2025, https://www.dictionary.com/browse/paralyze

we be willing to sit in that situation—being aware of it, recognizing it, yet still being okay.

How do you do that? It's all in *what* you choose to ponder.

Ponder God's goodness.

Ponder God's grace.

Ponder that God is still in control of everything.

Ponder God's faithfulness.

In the midst of your tough circumstances, don't be paralyzed. Move forward by choosing to ponder them in the light of God's amazing characteristics and promises.

Personal Reflection: Which describes you more—"paralyzed" or "pondering?" What would it look like to take steps out of paralyzed and into pondering? How can you begin doing that today?

_____

_____

_____

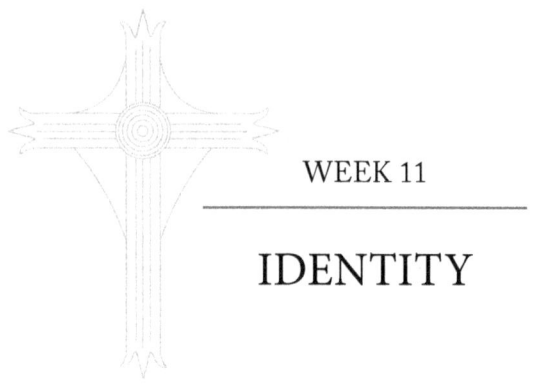

IDENTITY

John 1:12 - "Yet to all who did receive Him, to those who believed in His name, He gave the right to become children of God." (NIV)

What is your identity? I'm not just talking about your name—I'm asking what labels you give yourself, or what labels have been put on you. If you're not sure how to answer, think about these two questions. When you're looking in the mirror, what is it that you see? When you're introducing yourself to someone, what's the first thing you want them to know about you? Those things are what we put our identity in—the things that we choose to define us.

We all have places where we find our sense of identity, whether we like them or not. But what if the places where we look for our identities—or the ones given to us by others—aren't where our identity should truly lie?

I understand what it's like to have something you don't want become your identity. You know how I get people to remember me? I say this one thing: "Hi, I'm Jordan. I'm the one who's had the lung transplant."

Instantly, everyone remembers who I am. If I need to identify myself, that's how I do it. Having a transplant is such a large part of my life that I find myself talking about it to almost everyone. It's so controlling that everyone I meet has to know the limitations it puts on me. It's so all-encompassing that I can't tell you my story without explaining it. There are days when it seems to decide everything for me. How are things like that *not* our identity?

Maybe your identity is found in your job—how fast you can climb the ladder at work, or the letters written after your name. Having a job that you are proud of and working hard to achieve higher positions are not bad things, but should they be the only way we find value? Should they be what our worth is dependent upon?

Those labels, good and bad, are part of us, no doubt. We can't avoid them or escape them because they make up who we are. But as Christians, there is another identity that far surpasses *any* other label or identity we could use: *child of God.*

Your value lies in the fact that God loves you and made you in His image. He sent His only Son to die, suffer His wrath on your behalf, and rise from the grave to save those who believe in Him. There is no greater identity than being a beloved son or daughter of the Almighty God.

This should free us! Our worth is not in our jobs or our families (or whether or not we finish writing a devotional book). Our identity is not in our past failures or mistakes, health conditions we can't fix, or what people have said about us. We are a part of God's family through our faith in Jesus Christ.

The false identities you struggle with don't define you! God does. And 1 John 3:1 tells us how God defines us: "See what great love the Father has lavished on us, that we should be called children of God ..." (NIV)

Hear God saying this to you: "I created you. I define you. And what I see is my precious child!"

Personal Reflection: Write down the top three or four labels you put on yourself. Now, draw a single line through each one and write CHILD OF GOD in big letters beside it. Never forget that your identity lies in this alone.

_____

_____

_____

_____

_____

_____

_____

_____

_____

_____

_____

_____

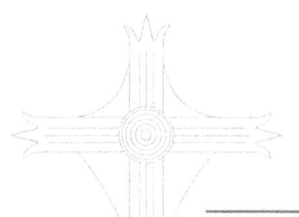

POWERFUL YET PERSONAL

Psalm 19:1 – "The heavens declare the glory of God; the skies proclaim the work of His hands." (NIV)

The beach is probably my favorite place on earth to be. Every year since I was young, my family and I have had the opportunity to go back to the same beach for a few days and just enjoy ourselves. Those are days I look forward to all year long. There's something amazing to me about walking along the beach, swimming in the ocean water … ahh, I am daydreaming about it now!

I wrote this poem while at the beach, late one night. I was sitting out on the balcony of the beachfront condo where we were staying, looking out over the water below and the stars above. I felt the cool breeze and listened to the waves crashing.

That's when it hit me: our God is *powerful!* He created all of those things. He created *everything.*

When I look at the ocean that endlessly stretches in each

direction and the stars that fill up the night sky, I feel really small. Do you? God hung each star and knows each one by name. Just think of the times in the Bible where He showed control over the sea—He parted it, He calmed it when it was raging, He walked on it. God is so powerful!

At the same moment, though, it also hit me that God is *personal.* That same all-powerful God desperately wants to have a relationship with us. That same all-powerful God knows your name and mine, walks beside us always, feels everything that we feel, and always thinks of us. We can't fully wrap our human minds around how personal such a powerful God can be, but it's true. Take time to reflect on that and thank God for it today.

How can the God who created the sea-
Still want to spend my life with me?
How can the God who numbered the stars-
Still long to have a place in my heart?
How can the God with no beginning nor end-
Still want to be called my best friend?
How can the God who took my place-
See all my mistakes yet still show me grace?
How can the God who watches over all-
Still be right there each time I call?
How can the God who sits up above-
Still make me feel this overwhelming love?
I don't understand this awesome King-
But for me, this God's changed everything.

Personal Reflection: In what ways do you see God showing you how powerful He is? In what ways does He show you how personal He is? Which do you tend to focus on more?

_____

_____

_____

_____

_____

_____

_____

_____

PUZZLE PIECES

Romans 8:28 - "And we know that in all things God works for the good of those who love Him, who have been called according to His purpose." (NIV)

Here's a crucial question for you. Do you like puzzles? I personally love them. It's become a tradition in my house to put a puzzle (or two!) together every year around the long Christmas break. My dad and I love to do them together, and my mom loves to pop in every once in a while when we get stuck and find the all-elusive missing piece.

At the very beginning of the puzzle, the first step is always to take all the pieces out of the box and dump them on the table. The most recent puzzle that we did started the same way. My dad dumped all the jumbled pieces onto the table, and I thought, "How can this turn into anything good? It's just a bunch of strange pieces that don't even look like they fit together!" The only thing that could prove me wrong was the picture on the box that showed what the finished product would be.

Then something occurred to me. That's the way life can feel sometimes! Do you ever look at your life and see just a bunch of pieces that don't seem to make any sense? Some seem to be broken, some don't fit anywhere, and some you hate so much you try to cover them up.

Sadly, we don't get the opportunity to see the "picture on the box" for our lives, so from our limited perspective, we can't see how all these pieces turn into anything good. We're just left seeing the mess. But God sees the whole puzzle! All the pieces make perfect sense to Him because He has designed them all.

Just like the people who make the puzzles that we put together for fun, God has handcrafted each piece to fit perfectly into our specific life-puzzles. Each person's life-puzzle will be different. Some pieces will make no sense to us. There are some pieces of my life that I would very happily forget about, throw in the trash, or keep anyone from ever seeing. But God has them all planned out for a reason.

So, what do we do when we can't see anything but the pieces? We trust God. We believe that even when we don't understand, He uses everything that we go through for our good and His glory.

Everything we experience is a piece in our puzzle. And, one day, when we reach Heaven, we will understand it all. We will see the finished product, and it will be a far greater, more beautiful picture than anything we could have imagined.

Lift all the pieces of your life up to God today, and trust that He is working them all together for good.

Personal Reflection: Reflect on a time when you've seen this play out in your life or a friend's life.

_____

_____

_____

_____

_____

_____

_____

_____

_____

_____

_____

_____

_____

_____

CONFIDENCE

Philippians 4:13 - "I can do all things through Christ who strengthens me." (NKJV)

I've never been a confident person. I've always felt like I'm the opposite, actually. Are you the same? Could it be, though, that our problem lies in what we are putting our confidence in?

Here is a funny illustration that will show you what I mean. I hate math. Have I mentioned this to you before? Probably, because I don't hide it well. Math has always been another language to me, one that I don't speak at all. My parents, on the other hand, love math. (That gene obviously skipped over me.) So, when I had to take a college math class, my poor mother (who has an engineering degree) had to tutor me.

My mother is the only reason that I got through that course. Before each of the five exams, I would be a complete nervous wreck. But my mom would very calmly look at me and say, "Jordan, you're prepared. I know you've done enough to get a good grade on this test." With that assurance from her, I would proceed with taking the exam. In the end, I received an A in the class!

But it wasn't just about the grade. I noticed something else along the way. I wasn't confident *at all* in *my* own abilities, whether that meant knowing the material or feeling prepared. My confidence only came when someone I trusted, my mother, told me I could do it.

God wants us to be confident not in ourselves or our own abilities, but in *Him*. Maybe you're someone like me, you're looking at the "test" before you, and all you can say is "I can't do this. I'm not good enough or prepared enough." Maybe you're struggling to have any confidence at all. If so, this verse should be so comforting for you and me.

We don't have to have confidence in our own abilities (or lack thereof!). We need to have confidence in *God*, remembering that because of Him, we can be strong and courageous because He is with us wherever we go.

Have confidence that if God calls you into something, He will give you what it takes to walk through it. Notice what the verse says: you can do all things *by His strength*. Not by your own power, not because you "believe in yourself" or "follow your heart," but because of Him.

We're only human. We are very limited. We may feel strong, but our own strength can only take us so far. We may feel able and determined, but those feelings will eventually fade. Confidence in ourselves will always leave us empty, wanting more. Confidence in the world, work, family, or friends will always leave us disappointed and struggling.

Instead, have confidence in *God* and trust that you can do whatever He calls you to. In *His* strength alone, you can face any test!

Personal Reflection: Are you feeling overwhelmed by a "test" in your life today? Could it be because you're having confidence in the wrong source?

_____

_____

_____

_____

_____

WEEK 15

CALL GOD

Jeremiah 33:3 - "Call to Me and I will answer you and tell you great and unsearchable things you do not know." (NIV)

I've got two questions to start off today: When something amazing happens to you, who is the first person that you want to tell? I'm talking about really great news—you just got engaged, you got the job you wanted, etc. Who's the first person that pops into your mind that you'd want to share it with? Got an answer? Okay.

The second question is the exact opposite. When something awful happens, something that breaks your heart or shakes you or scares you to death, who's the first person that you share *that* news with? It can be the same person for both answers. Got your answer in mind? Great.

Now, for either of those questions, was your answer God?

If you're suddenly feeling bad about your answers, don't. I didn't say God right away either. My first choices would be my parents and grandmother, and then, outside of family, probably my best friend. It's not wrong to share our circumstances with other people—after all, God calls us to fellowship with others. But we should all choose to share our celebrations and concerns with God first.

God truly desires to be the first one that we want to talk to about the good, bad, and in-between parts of life. Not because He doesn't already know or because we need to keep Him updated on our lives—He already knows everything that's going to happen in our lives. He wants us to come to Him first because He wants to have a relationship with us.

Remember who I named as my top people to reach out to? They were the first people I thought of because they are the ones that I'm closest to and have the best relationships with. I'm willing to bet yours is the same. But God wants to have that closeness, that relationship with us too.

A good friend recently shared an article with me about the verse above, Jeremiah 33:3. The article said that this verse is "God's phone number." I immediately thought, "Wow, wouldn't it be so cool if God actually had a phone number? You could just call Him up whenever you needed to talk!"

Then, it hit me: God is even closer than that. We don't need a phone to reach God! As believers, He is always with us and in us through His Holy Spirit.

So, the next time anything happens in your life, before you share it with anyone else, choose to "Call God" first. He's always ready and waiting to hear from us!

Personal Reflection: Try "calling God" this week, talking to Him first about everything. Write about how it went.

_____

_____

_____

_____

_____

_____

_____

_____

_____

_____

_____

_____

_____

_____

_____

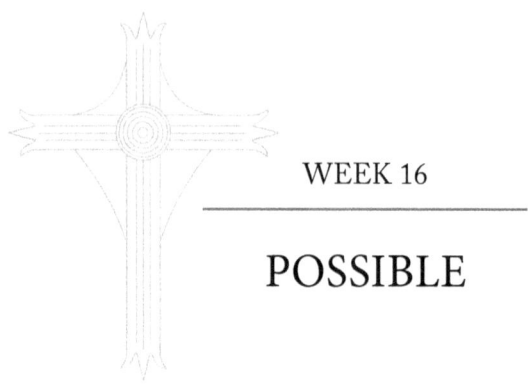

POSSIBLE

1 Corinthians 16:13 - "... stand firm in the faith ..."
(NIV)

Wₑ have a plaque in our kitchen, right underneath our microwave, that reads, "Faith does not make things easy; it makes things possible." I don't know where or even when we got it, but I took extra notice of it one day and started to think about that idea.

Has anyone ever told you that being a Christian should make your life easier? Maybe someone even said that if you were a stronger Christian, things would have gone better for you. Maybe they suggested that if you'd prayed harder or read your Bible more, you wouldn't have struggled. Maybe they said you're just not "the right kind of Christian," or else God would have cleared the path so that everything would have gone perfectly.

If someone has ever told you any of these things, take heart—they are not true! Those are all false ideas, and if we look to the Bible, we will see that God never told us any of them.

What would Jesus say in response to those words? I believe, if He were here responding to them right now, He would very graciously and kindly look at us and say, "Do you think dying on the cross was easy for Me?"

In fact, anyone who thinks that life should be easy just because we have faith is completely overlooking or misunderstanding the entire concept of Christianity. In John 16:33, Jesus *guaranteed* we would have trouble in this world. He felt it personally in becoming sin for us, experiencing the torture of the Cross, and worst of all, enduring separation from His Father. So, it stands to reason that if life was hard for Christ, life on this side of Heaven will not be easy for us.

So, what does faith do? It makes things *possible*.

Faith puts our focus back on God.

Faith reminds us He has already overcome the world.

Faith shows us that He is holding onto us, walking through the struggle with us.

Faith gives us the hope of Heaven.

Faith does not make things easy. It doesn't remove the obstacles or take away the pain we feel in life. Tragedies still happen; we still feel hurt. Faith doesn't take you out of the painful situations … but it gives you what you need to survive in them.

Faith in God doesn't make it all easy. It makes it all *possible*.

Personal Reflection: Meditate on my plaque's words this week, and write what it means to you that faith makes things possible.

_____

_____

_____

_____

_____

_____

_____

_____

_____

_____

_____

_____

_____

_____

_____

TREASURE

Psalm 119:162 - "I rejoice at Your word as one who finds great treasure." (NKJV)

In the 1850s, there was a huge gold rush in Montana. A group of men found a large amount of gold in a river, but they were too low on supplies to gather the gold at that moment and would have to go back into town to make purchases first. They didn't want anyone in town to know about this gold, so they made a pact. They would go back into town to get what they needed, but they would tell no one.

Ten days later, they left the town to go back for the gold. There was a small problem, though ... fifty people from the town followed them! All the men asked the same question: who told? But the answer was no one.

So, how did so many townspeople know about the treasure they'd found? Because of the way they acted! One of the townspeople said it was the smile on the men's faces that gave it away. The men didn't have to say a single word because their expressions and actions said it all. They had found a treasure that was so great they couldn't hide how it made them feel!

As Christians, we have a treasure that is *way* more valuable than any gold those men could have possibly discovered. But instead of making a pact to keep it a secret, God calls us in Matthew 28:19 to do the opposite –"go and make disciples of all nations" (NIV).

We have the treasure of Jesus in us, with us, for us. We have the treasure of eternal life in Heaven. We have the treasure of God's word. These treasures last forever, long after gold ever will.

What if you acted like it? What would change in your life if you started to live like you had that incredible treasure?

I'm not saying we need to constantly be jumping for joy through every moment. I'll be the first to tell you I'm not always in a celebratory mood. It doesn't make us bad Christians or lesser people if we have moments where we cry instead of smile. This treasure doesn't keep me from worrying before a big test or breaking down in tears over the death of a loved one. But even in those moments, we should hold onto this treasure that we have, letting the amazing benefits of Christ change our perspectives.

The way we act should reveal what we believe. We should let others see the treasure we have inside us. Let them see we are different, and let them follow us to where our treasure lies.

Personal Reflection: Do you truly believe you've discovered the most amazing treasure? What would change if you spent this week acting like it?

_____

_____

_____

_____

_____

_____

_____

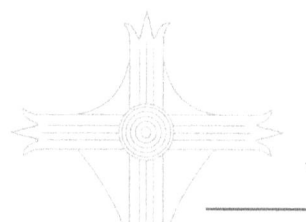

WEEK 18

BLESSINGS VS. BURDENS

Psalm 103:2 - "Bless the Lord, O my soul, and forget not all His benefits" (NKJV)

I think most of us are familiar with the famous hymn "Count Your Many Blessings." I used to sing a duet of it often with a good friend of mine, and that special time always brought me joy. The words talk about how important it is to list each of the many blessings God has given us … but isn't it easier sometimes to name all the burdens we're carrying instead?

When I say "count," I don't just mean numerically. (I might have gotten an A in that math class, but I still don't like numbers!) It also means to focus on, think about most, give our attention to something. We ultimately focus on one or the other—the blessings or the burdens.

The definition of *blessing* is "a favor or gift bestowed by God …"[4] By contrast, a *burden* is a load that is "borne

---

4. *Dictionary.com*, s.v. "blessing," accessed August 3, 2025, https://www.dictionary.com/browse/blessing

with difficulty"[5] (like the bag you filled up in our earlier exercise!).

Which one is it for you? In the quiet moments when you're alone, what does your mind go to? The good things in your life or the bad?

I'm willing to bet that wherever you are in life right now, you have plenty of both. These definitions made me realize that focusing on one automatically lifts us up, while focusing on the other automatically holds us down. Counting blessings lets us look up to see the light and how God is active in our day-to-day lives. But counting burdens keeps us weighed down in darkness and wondering where God is.

Which one does God want us to count? I think the answer to that is pretty clear! He wants us to focus on the blessings and gifts He's given us. He's so kind and gracious, giving us so many gifts every day that we take for granted. Choose to focus on those instead of the burdens you're carrying.

I'm not telling you to pretend the burdens aren't there. They're real and hard and painful. But God wants us to give *Him* our burdens so we can be free to rejoice in all He has done.

Years ago, I started setting aside time every night, right before bed, to list out ten blessings from my day and thank God for them. What I learned through that nightly routine is that no matter how bad I thought my day was, I could always find at least ten gifts God had given me.

---

5. *Dictionary.com* s.v. "burden," accessed August 3, 2025, https://www.dictionary.com/browse/burden

Make a list of all the blessings in your life. Meditate on them and thank Him for all of them. You just might find that doing this helps remind you Who is holding all your burdens. Make the conscious choice to thank God for everything He's given you today. Choose to count your blessings.

Personal Reflection: List out ten blessings from your day today. Then, do the same each day this week. (Don't repeat any you wrote on a previous day—this will challenge you to look for even more blessing to count!)

_____

_____

_____

_____

_____

_____

_____

_____

_____

_____

_____

_____

_____

_____

FEAR NOT

Isaiah 41:10 – "So do not fear, for I am with you; do not be dismayed, for I am your God ..." (NIV)

I will be completely honest with you here. If you were to ask me what my number one struggle is in my Christian walk, I would probably say fear. I don't admit this very often or very easily, but it's true.

Is it the same for you? What areas do you feel it most in your life? Are you like me and feel it way more than you wish you did? If so, let me tell you some of the things that God has to say about our fears. I need these reminders regularly.

First, we don't have to be controlled by fear. Fear shouldn't own us. It shouldn't make all our decisions or captivate our thoughts or be what defines us. As we've already seen, the only thing that defines us or captivates us should be God alone.

Fear also isn't from God; it's from Satan. God hates seeing us drowning in all the fears we carry. Now, this does *not* mean that your fears aren't valid. They're very real, and we can't just wish them away. So, what do we do with them? We give them over to God, who wants to carry them for us. Things may look scary, but He has everything under control. We can give all our fears to Him, place our trust in Him, and know that He's got us in His loving hands.

I want to add just a few more Bible verses that talk about our ongoing battle with fear to end for today. Meditate on these words. Hold onto these beautiful promises. No matter what happens in your life, God is graciously telling you every day, *do not fear.*

Psalm 118:6 – "The Lord is with me; I will not be afraid ..."

John 14:27 – "Peace I leave with you; my peace I give you ... Do not let your hearts be troubled and do not be afraid."

Deuteronomy 3:22 – "Do not be afraid of them; the Lord your God himself will fight for you."

Lamentations 3:57 – "You came near when I called you, and you said, 'Do not fear.'"

Personal Reflection: Make your own list of Fear Not verses that speak to you the most.

_____

_____

_____

_____

_____

_____

_____

HOLD THEM UP

Galatians 6:2 - "Carry each other's burdens, and in this way you will fulfill the law of Christ." (NIV)

Jesus says very clearly how important it is to Him that we as Christians help those around us. He calls "loving our neighbor" one of the most important commandments (Matthew 22:38-39). But what does that really look like? How do we really go about doing it on a practical level? I often think of this story from Exodus 17, which gives us a clear picture of what it means to literally hold someone up in the midst of a struggle.

Moses, the leader of the Israelites, was watching his Israelite army fight a battle against the Amalekites, an enemy of the nation of Israel. As he watched the battle rage from a nearby hill, he noticed something. When Moses had his hands raised to God, the Israelites were winning the battle! But when his hands were lowered, the Israelites began losing. He knew he had to keep his hands raised the entire duration of the battle for the Israelites to claim the victory.

Have you ever tried to keep your hands up for any amount of time? I have, and I only get about one minute in before my arms start getting tired. Can you imagine having to do that for hours? As you can guess, Moses got tired and reached a point where he couldn't do it anymore. But then, Aaron and Hur, Moses' brother and nephew, literally held his weary arms up for him. Each took one of his arms and kept it pointed toward God until the battle was over. The Israelites won!

We all know people who are tired of the fight, who are weary physically, mentally, and spiritually. What do we choose to do in those situations? We can choose to walk past those people and be focused only on our own problems, or we can choose to be like Aaron and Hur. We can come beside the person who is hurting, and we can lift them up. We can point them toward God. We can encourage them; we can help them.

I don't know why God chose to make the battle unfold like that any more than I know why people around me are fighting their own battles. I wish I could change it for them, make it easier, or take it away, but I can't. I can't fight their battle *for* them, but I can fight it *with* them. I can support them. I can come alongside them and let them know they are never alone.

I can't put into words how many times friends have done this for me or how grateful I am for it. We all need to be "held up" by others. And we all have the ability to hold others up as well. Who will you choose to find and help today?

Personal Reflection: Who in your life needs to be "held up?" Choose to help them this week.

_____

_____

_____

_____

_____

_____

_____

_____

_____

_____

_____

_____

_____

_____

WEEK 21

MIRACLES

Psalm 77:14 - "You are the God who performs miracles..." (NIV)

"I t's a miracle!" We often use this phrase, typically with a mocking tone of voice, when something surprisingly good happens. We say it flippantly, but do we ever really think about how many miracles actually do surround us?

It's easy for us to look in the Bible and see Red-Sea-parting moments or Feeding-of-Five-Thousand moments and label them "miracles." But do we recognize miracles today, or do we miss them? Do the bigger miracles that demand a response get labels like "coincidence" or "fate" or just attributed to society's advancements, while the less-noticeable miracles just pass right by without us thinking about them?

This poem was written from a perspective of wanting my eyes to be opened to all the miracles God does for me that I *don't* see. Take a second and listen to your heartbeat. Each one is a miracle that God chose to perform in your life!

Listen to each breath you take. That's a miracle too! Did you wake up this morning? Miracle. Did you see the sun and the birds, or maybe you're reading this in winter and see a million snowflakes falling? All miracles.

Miracles didn't end when the stories in the Bible ended—they're all around us! We've just lost our ability to recognize them. I don't want to miss the miracles and the gifts that God gives me all throughout every day. I want to accept each one as the incredible blessing that it is.

I started this devotional with a saying, and I'll end with another. This is one that my dad says all the time, and I just smile in agreement every time I hear him say it: "God is still in the business of doing miracles." Look for them, celebrate them, and then, praise God for them!

Miracles surround us; they're never far
We just have to see them for what they are
They aren't just stories from days of old
They're current stories that should be told
Each beat of your heart; each breath you take
Each and every morning when you awake
Every sunrise and every sunset
The love you feel; the joy you get
Peace when your mind should be racing
Family and friends warmly embracing
Miracles surround us; they're never far
Never forget how special they are

Personal Reflection: Try looking for miracles, big and small, this week. Then, write down how many you find.

MORE

Psalm 113:4 - "The Lord is high above all nations, His glory above the heavens." (NKJV)

I got the opportunity a few years ago to lead a group of incredible young women through a one-week Christian conference. During that time, one of the questions that I asked each one of them was, "How do you picture God?" In other words, when you think of God, what comes to your mind?

I loved hearing each of the girls' answers. Each one was beautiful and unique. What would your answer be? Also, along those same lines, what attributes of God do you value most?

I'll give you my answers to these questions, which will hopefully clarify what I mean. When I picture God, I picture the sun's rays or a lit cross, and the attribute of God that means the most to me is probably His faithfulness. In any and all circumstances, He is faithful. Those are my answers—got yours?

Now, here's the best part. God is so much *more* than what you're envisioning! It makes me think of those TV commercials where after you've endured seemingly endless minutes of the actual advertisement, the narrator exclaims, "But wait! There's *more!*" I feel like that's what God is saying to us (but in this case, it's a good thing!).

What do you think God is? Faithful? Merciful? Graceful? Sovereign? Mighty? Guess what—there's more! God is so much more than anything we can imagine. In fact, He's not just more *of* any attribute we can imagine; He is also more *than* any attribute we can imagine. Ephesians 3:20 describes God as being able to do "*immeasurably* more than all we ask or imagine" (NIV).

We won't fully see or understand it all until we get to Heaven. Not because He's trying to hide from us, but because He's so great that our limited human minds couldn't possibly take it all in. God is always wanting to reveal new parts of Himself to us if we're open to them. He can use any season we are in to do this, but I've noticed throughout my life that it's the hard times and bad situations where I learn something new about God. I can clearly look back on really tough moments and point you to exactly where God taught me something about Himself, and I try to carry those lessons with me.

What about you? Think back on your life—can you see how God has shown you new parts of Himself through good moments or bad ones? Whatever moment you're in right now, is there something about Himself that He's trying to get you to see?

Hold onto those things and picture God smiling and telling you, "But wait—there's so much more!"

Personal Reflection: What do you picture when you think of God? What's the most important attribute to you? Is God trying to show you something more about Himself?

_____

_____

_____

_____

_____

_____

_____

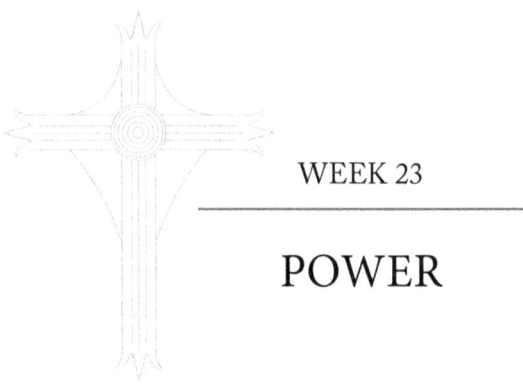

POWER

1 Chronicles 29:11 - "Yours, Lord, is the greatness and the power ..." (NIV)

Here's a sentence I never thought I'd say: I've survived a hurricane! I live in a part of Georgia that got a direct hit from Hurricane Helene. In fact, as a little behind-the-scenes for you, I'm writing this devotional on my phone right now (instead of my computer) because the storm knocked out our internet, and it still isn't restored yet. (Hopefully there won't be any typos from using such a smaller device—thank goodness for spell check!)

My mom, myself, and our dog, Lily, sat in our bathtub, the only safe place we could think of in our house, for three hours while the Category 1 hurricane barreled through our town. I've never experienced anything like it, and I'm still reeling from it all. As I sat there listening to the 100-miles-per-hour winds and the pouring rain, something hit me: I had absolutely no power. No, I'm not talking about power as in electricity, though we didn't have any of that for a while either. I'm talking about the power to control the situation.

We (or at least I) try so hard to control everything around us. Sometimes we even get the illusion that we *are* in control. But then there are moments when we all get hit hard by the tough truth that we can't control anything. There I was, sitting in the tub, knowing I couldn't control the storm. I couldn't protect my family from it or keep it from hitting my house. I was powerless. Isn't that terrifying? It certainly was for me. My family will tell you I screamed a lot that night.

What's that moment for you?

But as Christians, the fact that we have no control shouldn't scare us. Why? Because we know who has control of everything. God has *all* power in Heaven and on earth. We acknowledge this when we pray the Lord's Prayer. When we say this prayer to God, we say His "is the kingdom and the *power* and the glory forever" (Matt 6:13 NKJV).

He had power over the storm I was experiencing in the bathtub all night. He has power over the storm you're in too. He may choose to calm the storm in your life, or He may allow it to give you a direct hit and leave you reeling from it. But either way, He has control over it. He has more power than it does. In His perfect plan, He's orchestrating all of it.

Will you choose to trust in the God who has all power and all control today? You have none. I have none. Instead of letting that scare us, though, let it stir us to draw closer to the One who has it all.

Personal Reflection: Are you in a "storm" making you feel powerless right now? If so, write about it. If not, write about a time when you were. How does it comfort you to know God is in control of your storm?

_____

_____

_____

_____

_____

_____

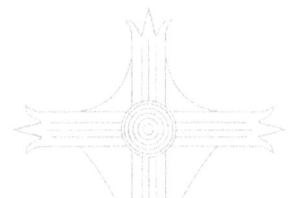

COUNTING GOD-THOUGHTS

Hebrews 3:1 - "Therefore, holy brothers and sisters, who share in the heavenly calling, fix your thoughts on Jesus ..." (NIV)

How many times have you thought about God today? Seriously—take a second to come up with a number. For me, (not counting the time I've spent thinking about this devotional, to be fair) I would say I've probably thought of God three or four times. It's two p.m. right now. Those are just instances where I've *thought* about God, not talked to or spent time with Him. Sadly, that number would be lower. What about you?

We have a sign in our foyer, right by our front door, that reads:

> *"In happy moments, praise God.*
> *In difficult moments, seek God.*
> *In quiet moments, worship God.*
> *In every moment, thank God."*

Did you catch that there are lots of changing moments in there? After all, life is full of changing circumstances. But did you notice what doesn't change, no matter what? Our focus. No matter the moment, our focus should always stay on God!

Think of an example of each of these in your life. How do you respond? Do you keep your focus on God? I'll share mine with you so you see where I'm going here.

The first is "happy moments." I'm probably my very happiest at the beach! When I'm at the beach, looking out at the ocean, do I choose to praise God in that happy moment? Or do I fail to thank Him for His marvelous creation?

When I think of "difficult moments," I think of the medical challenges of my transplant life. When I'm in the hospital doing tests all day, for example, do I choose to seek God? Or do I spend the day in fear?

In a "quiet moment," like when I'm getting ready for bed, do I worship God? Or do I turn on the TV or go on my phone?

I find that I often choose not to think of God. Do you? The more we love God, the more we should desire to think about Him. Think of someone you love very deeply—don't you enjoy thinking of them, being with them, and talking with them? As the moments in our lives come and go, as they constantly change, try to focus on the God who never changes and know that He is always thinking of you. That's the kind of love He has for you. He's always with you, thinking of you, hoping you will think of Him.

Personal Reflection: Be aware of how many times you think about God this week. Then, try to move toward thinking of Him in everything. Write about how it goes.

_____

_____

_____

_____

_____

_____

_____

_____

_____

_____

_____

_____

_____

_____

_____

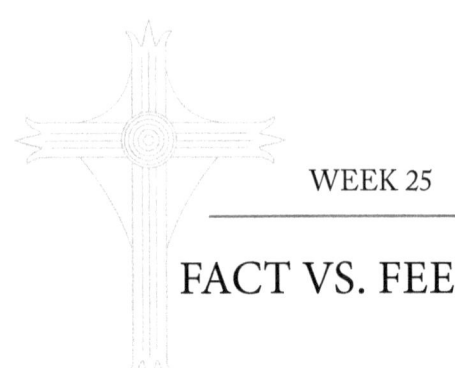

FACT VS. FEELING

Proverbs 28:26 – "He who trusts in his own heart is a fool, but whoever walks wisely will be delivered."
(NKJV)

It's time for another word-comparison. Let's just dive right in with our two words for today: *fact* and *feeling*. What do you think the differences are between them?

A *fact* is defined as "something known to be true."[6] A *feeling* is "an emotion or emotional perception."[7]

Both of them will show up in every situation that you come across. The problem is facts and feelings often compete with each other. They often contradict each other. So, which one do we listen to? When they both try to pull us in separate directions, which do we follow?

Let me give you a funny example. I have a very strange but

6. *Dictionary.com*, s.v. "fact," accessed August 3, 2025, https://www.dictionary.com/browse/fact
7. *Dictionary.com*, s.v. "feeling," accessed August 3, 2025, https://www.dictionary.com/browse/feeling

serious fear of most bugs. Especially cockroaches, which are frequently found where I live. My *feeling* about cockroaches is that they must be evil. If one is in the kitchen, it can have the entire room. I'm leaving!

That's my emotional reaction. The *fact* is that while they're huge, they don't have the power to harm me since I'm about a million times bigger than they are. That's what's *true*.

Do you see how facts and feelings are opposites? That was a funny example that was meant to make you laugh, but most of the time these moments aren't funny at all. Some people's feelings tell them they don't deserve to live anymore. Some tell them they aren't lovable, or that God's abandoned them. What hard things do your feelings tell you?

There are two kinds of people. The first is the people we've just been talking about, who need a message like this because they desperately hope their *feelings* aren't *facts*. That's the kind of person that I am. I love hearing about the difference between the two because often my feelings don't tell me good things. I hate the idea of having to trust my feelings, so this is a comforting message. Are you like me?

The second group is people who need a message like this because they trust their own feelings too much. Let me be clear—feelings aren't bad. God gave us hearts and emotions, but He has also given us facts, and we get in trouble when we think our feelings and instincts are more trustworthy and reliable.

If you're one of these people, this is probably a confronting message for you. If so, consider this question: Doesn't that put you in place of God? Doesn't that make your perspective suddenly of more value to you than God's?

After hearing all this, maybe you're wondering where you can go to actually find the facts. The answer is that we should go directly to the Bible to find facts and words of truth that God wants us to hear!

Let me give you some facts from God's word that you can always rely on, no matter what, to get you started:

You are LOVED by God (Rom. 5:8). You are His perfect creation (Gen. 1:27). You are made, known, and treasured by Him (Ps. 139:13-14). He is with you always (Deut. 31:6). He is in control (Prov. 19:21). He is always faithful (Deut. 7:9).

Personal Reflection: Which of the two categories (people who hope their feelings aren't fact or people who rely too much on feelings) are you? Based on your answer, what does this devotional mean to you?

_____

_____

_____

_____

_____

_____

_____

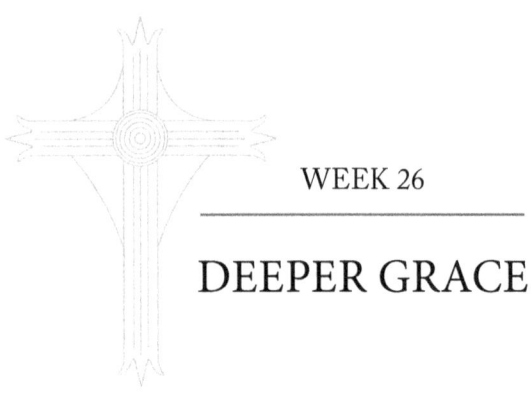

WEEK 26

DEEPER GRACE

*John 1:16 - "For of His fullness we have all received ...
grace upon grace." (NASB)*

We've officially made it halfway through this book
together! Thanks for sticking with me—I'm praying
it's been a blessing to you. To celebrate the halfway mark, I
wanted this devotional to be a special one. So, I'm going to
share a more personal message and a new piece of my story.

There was a time when I got the opportunity to think about
this question: If there were one thing I wanted people to
know about my life, what would it be? I didn't know how
to answer for a little while, until I heard something a pastor
said. He was saying a prayer before the start of his sermon,
and one line of that prayer would end up being something
I'll never forget.

He was praying for those who were sick in his congregation,
and he asked that God would show them a "deeper measure
of grace." In that moment, it was like God opened my eyes
to see how that's what has surrounded my life from day

one: a deep measure of God's *grace*. Yes, grace to keep me physically alive against all odds, but also grace to keep me going emotionally through all the ups and downs. I could share countless stories with you to prove this point, but there is one in particular that illustrates what I mean.

It had been a really hard stretch of time for my health. Things were just not going well, and I had an early morning medical test that I just knew wouldn't give me good news. To make matters worse, the *entire* night before, I hadn't slept at all due to another separate health issue (and that not sleeping thing had become pretty normal at that point). I was tired, worried, frustrated, and just done.

I love music, and my all-time favorite song, aside from ones I've helped write with a close friend, is "God Who Stays" by Matthew West. That song was written a few years ago, and because Matthew West has written so many more songs since then, it is rarely ever on the radio anymore. But on the thirty-minute drive down to the hospital that difficult morning, I heard it on the radio *twice!*

Some might say it was just a little thing or pass it off as coincidence (or maybe even hallucinations due to my sleep-deprivation). But I knew it was more. I could feel God with me in that moment, and I knew He was comforting me. He knew how much that song would mean, and He was helping me through that tough day.

That's a deeper measure of grace. But it's not just grace—it's unbelievable kindness as well. I believe that the harder our paths, the more God covers that path in His *grace*. Look for those gifts in your own life … and thank God for the *deep grace* and *unending kindness* He shows!

Personal Reflection: You just heard my story of God's kindness and grace—what's yours? Write out your story of when God showed a deeper measure of grace to you.

_____

_____

_____

_____

_____

_____

_____

_____

_____

_____

_____

_____

_____

DEEP END FAITH

Hebrews 11:6 - "And without faith it is impossible to please God ..." (NIV)

How deep do you think your faith is? Think about that as we walk through today's devotional because I want to talk about different types of faith.

For the analogy we're about to use, water is going to represent faith. Imagine a drinking-glass-sized jar filled with water. Some people have a faith level that's about this size. They keep it sitting on a shelf most of the time, and maybe every once in a while, they'll carry it around or splash a little on themselves, but not much more than that. With that amount of faith, you can't do much.

But I want to be clear—if you're a new Christian starting out in your faith journey, this kind of faith is a good place to start! God says the faith of a mustard seed can move mountains. But God doesn't call us to *stay* in that spot of "waterglass" faith.

Now imagine the shallow end of a pool. Some people have "shallow end" faith. These people feel comfortable walking in faith, even being submerged in it … but only to a point. Their feet still have to be on the ground.

You can do some things in the shallow end of a pool, right? You can play around some. You can float. But there's a limit to the shallow end. You certainly can't swim in it very well. If you're stuck in the shallow end, think of all the places that you can't go and all the things you can't do in the pool. You're limited in your abilities.

Finally, envision the deep end of a swimming pool. This is the kind of faith God calls us to have! My grandfather renamed it appropriately, calling it "*Depend* faith!" That means that we trust and *depend* on God with our entire being, we are *fully submerged* in faith. When we can't see the bottom, there appears to be no solid ground under us. We have no control. Yet we choose to have complete faith. That's the kind of faith He calls us to have and what He can use the most.

Which category are you in? I'm probably in the "shallow end" faith, if I'm being honest, though I try daily to move deeper. No matter which kind of faith you have, hear God calling out to you from the deep end, urging you to go deeper with Him. Just like a little kid diving into the pool for the first time with a mom or dad waiting nearby with open arms, hear Him repeating the words, *"I've got you."* Wherever you find yourself, take steps forward toward a deeper faith in God today.

Personal Reflection: What faith category are you in? Is that the category God wants you to be in? How can you move deeper?

GOD IS BIGGER

John 16:33 - "I have told you these things, so that in Me you may have peace. In this world you will have trouble. But take heart! I have overcome the world." *(NIV)*

Do you ever feel like you're just too small, and your situation is just too big? I certainly understand that overwhelming feeling, but something my mom said once got me thinking about it in a whole different way.

We had just found out some bad news about a family that we knew. An unexpected tragedy had left part of the family reeling and devastated. My mom's prayer for that sweet family was, "God, please show them that You are bigger than these circumstances in their lives." That stuck with me. The more I thought about it, the more I realized she was right. We all need to be reminded that God is bigger than the big obstacles we are facing.

We don't have to look hard to find people in the Bible who were facing big circumstances. The Bible is filled with stories of people who were struggling with horrible difficulties that were way too big for them to handle. But besides those big obstacles, they all had something else in common.

They all had *God*. They all had faith that God was bigger. Think about it …

Daniel saw that God was bigger than a den full of hungry lions.

Joseph saw that God was bigger than false accusations, wrongful imprisonment, and horrible treatment.

David saw that God was bigger than a literal giant.

Shadrach, Meshach, and Abednego saw that God was bigger than the fire they were thrown into.

Job saw that God was bigger than unimaginable pain and loss.

You could go on and on finding Biblical figures who were faced with huge trials. But each one persevered, not because of their own strength, but because they knew they had a God with them that was *bigger* than it all.

What's your story? What big things are you fighting with today? Take comfort in knowing that whatever they are, our God is so much bigger. He has ultimately overcome every trouble and trial we will ever face, because *He has overcome the world.*

Personal Reflection: *In what areas of your life do you need to be reminded that "God is bigger" today? Fill in your own story: _____ saw that God is bigger than _____!*

_____

_____

_____

_____

_____

_____

_____

_____

_____

_____

_____

_____

_____

THORNS

2 Corinthians 12:9 - "But [God] said to me, 'My grace is sufficient for you, for My power is made perfect in weakness.' Therefore I will boast all the more gladly about my weaknesses, so that Christ's power may rest on me." (NIV)

The man who wrote these words was Paul. After God changed his heart, Paul did many incredible things for the kingdom of God. In fact, he was one of the most important figures in the history of Christianity.

Years into his Christian ministry, he was given what he described as a "thorn in his flesh" (2 Cor. 12:7). We aren't told any more details of what this thorn was, but we know it was more than just a little hindrance. It was so hard on him that he pleaded with God three separate times to remove it in 2 Corinthians 12:8. But God chose not to.

What Paul writes in the next verse blows my mind. God's answer to Paul's pleadings was "no," but instead of just leaving Paul with that, He reassured Paul by saying His power would be made perfect even in the weakness that Paul desperately wanted removed!

Look at the shift in Paul's heart and mind after that response. He goes from begging God to remove the thorn to saying he's going to *boast* about it. *Wow!*

What's your "thorn?" I can think of a few in my life, but one that I have dealt with ever since I was young is migraines. I always really struggled with them because they didn't seem to have any good purpose. With my health or other struggles I've had, I could at least see where God could use them, but the migraines seemed to only be used for driving me insane. I couldn't see any good at all coming out of them … just canceled plans and hours spent lying in a dark bedroom.

So, how do we reach the same conclusion that Paul did with the thorns that we have?

We need to start by recognizing that God says He works *everything* together for the good of those who love Him and are called according to His purpose (Rom. 8:28). This verse states it pretty clearly: everything we go through has a purpose. We might not see it, but God promises that nothing is wasted. The purpose might be to draw us closer to Him, get us to depend on Him more, get our attention, or show us that He is in control. Maybe we'll see new purposes down the road, or maybe we won't see them until Heaven.

Whatever thorn you are dealing with today, let's both try to get to the point Paul did, where we can confidently trust that God will use any and all of them for His glory and our good.

Personal Reflection: How do Paul's words here show how God is working on his heart with his thorn? Are you willing to say the same about the thorns in your life?

_____

_____

_____

_____

_____

_____

_____

WEEK 30

GOD'S TIME

Psalm 37:7 - "Be still before the Lord and wait patiently for Him ..." (NIV)

It's very hard to wait. Have you ever noticed that? One of my favorite quotes is "God, give me patience—but *hurry up!*"

Are you in a season of waiting right now? Maybe it's just in one or two small areas of your life, or maybe you feel like it's your entire life, like you're just waiting for something to give, for things to make sense, for things to change. If that's you, I hope you are helped by these three important concepts that God has shown me when it comes to seasons of waiting:

First, *God's timing is what we want.* We need to realize and truly believe that. As Christians, we want to be in the center of His will, right? If that's the case, then we should want to be in the center of His timing as well.

God's the only One who sees the future. God's the only

One with a perfect plan He's orchestrating for your life. Therefore, if it's not God's timing, we ultimately don't want it. If God blocked that one path, we don't want to go down it.

Second, *God is always on time.* The hard part is that this might not be *our* time. His timing might make absolutely no sense to us and leave us reeling, but He's still on time. His time. His perfect time.

I'm the kind of person who always feels like I should take charge in this area. I have my timetable, which seems perfectly reasonable to me. It works great for me, and I feel like I need to organize it all and then present it to God. It's as if I'm saying "Okay God, I've done all this work for You. Here's the plan, now just make it happen." But it's not up to me to do that.

A friend once sent me this saying: "When it's not in God's time, you can't force it. When it is in God's time you can't stop it." I love that, but I always thought it should say, "When it's not in God's time you *shouldn't* force it." We still try to force it anyway. But we shouldn't. His timetable is so much better.

Finally, it's okay to recognize, as we already have, that this is *hard.* God knows that too. Psalm 27:14 says, "Wait for the Lord; be strong and take heart …" (NIV). Scripture recognizes that it takes strength to do this. It takes courage. It takes faith to wait and persevere and keep hoping.

Let me end with this promise from Scripture for those who do strive to wait for the Lord:

Isaiah 40:31 - "But those who wait on the Lord shall renew their strength; they shall mount up with wings like eagles, they shall run and not be weary, they shall walk and not faint." (NKJV)

Personal Reflection: What are you waiting for today? Read over my friend's saying again—what does that mean in your life?

_____

_____

_____

_____

_____

_____

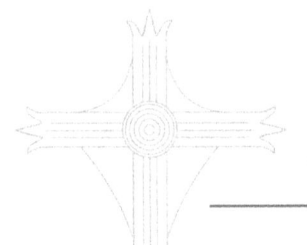

F.R.O.G.

Proverbs 3:5-6 - "Trust in the Lord with all your heart and lean not on your own understanding; in all your ways submit to Him, and He will make your paths straight." (NIV)

Are you already wondering about the title of this devotional? I don't blame you. First off, I like frogs—you can call me crazy, but I think they're cute. But we're talking about something totally different here: today, **FROG** is an acronym. It stands for **F**ully **R**ely **O**n **G**od. Let's begin by looking at the following Bible verses that all relate to our topic:

Ps. 37:5 - "Commit your way to the Lord ..."

Ps.55:22 - "Cast your cares on the Lord and He will sustain you; He will never let the righteous be shaken."

Ps. 56:3 - "When I am afraid, I put my trust in You."

Is. 26:4 - "Trust in the Lord forever, for the Lord, the Lord Himself, is the Rock eternal."

All these verses come down to the acronym *Fully Rely On God*. Each one gives us a command to and/or a reason why we should **FROG**. These are just a few examples of all the times in the Bible that God speaks about relying on Him.

The very first verse that I listed at the top of this page, Proverbs 3:5-6, is my mom's favorite verse. Every single day, I see her personify the entire idea of relying on God alone. That's why this verse means so much to her. Through everything that she's had to face, she has learned to rely on only God. That means not relying on her own strengths or smarts or the doctors who were there during medical crises. Not relying on family or friends to fix her grieving heart. Not relying on statistics or odds, whether they're in her favor or not. In all these ways, she illustrates the importance of trusting in the Lord, not her own understanding.

There are so many things in this world that we rely on. But what does it mean to rely on God? It means to trust Him alone. We must believe in everything He has said in His Word, giving Him all our worries and cares and desires and surrendering them all to His will. It means that in everything we do, we must *submit to Him,* doing what He would want us to. It's a complete life-change when we make the decision to **FROG**.

So why do we choose to rely only on God? Because He's the only one in all of this world who will *never let anyone down*. He's got the perfect plan for each of us, and as His followers, we are called to trust Him no matter what.

He's got you! You can count on it. So, whatever you are facing today, make the decision in your heart to **FROG**!

Personal Reflection: What/who do you rely on? Try to **FROG** *this week and write about what happens.*

_____

_____

_____

_____

_____

_____

OUT-LOVE

1 Peter 4:8 - "Above all, love each other deeply ..."
(NIV)

I heard someone say once that "You'll never look someone in the eyes that God doesn't love." What does that phrase actually mean?

Another way to say it is that God loves every single person that we see ... because God loves *every single person*. John 3:16, which most of us are familiar with, tells us this: "For God so *loved* the world that he gave His one and only Son ..." The people that you see might not know He loves them. They might reject that love. They might not love Him back—in fact, they might hate Him. But that doesn't change that He loves them.

Think about the significance of that. God loves every person that you see. How many people do you see throughout your day? At work or at the grocery store or just around your town? As I've shared before, I'm not around people very often because of my health. But I'll give you an example from one of the rare times that I was.

I've had the opportunity to visit the Augusta National Golf Tournament a few times. Anyone who is familiar with that knows how popular and crowded it is. Maybe it's just because I'm not used to being around large groups, but I'm always blown away by how many people are there. What's the largest crowd you've ever been in? God loves each of those people. He knows every detail of each of their lives. He hears each one when they pray.

Jesus died for each one of them. That's how much He loves each and every one of us. Isn't that amazing?

So, how should we respond? First, it should overwhelm us. (In a good way, though.) It should make us grateful and humbled. We should want to love God more, and it should encourage us to show everyone His amazing love. Why? Because we're called to be His ambassadors and represent Him.

But what about those people who are hard to love? You know the ones—those who just don't show you any kindness or whom you can't get along with, no matter how hard you try. As my mom would say, we're called to out-love them.

What does that mean? It means show kindness, even when it's not shown back to you. After all, this is how Jesus loves. Even if they don't respond to it, you must love them even more. Everyone is made in God's image, which means everyone is valuable. Make it a personal, spiritual challenge to find someone you can out-love today. Who will it be for you?

"You'll never look someone in the eyes that God doesn't love." Let's try to say the same about each of us—that we never look someone in the eyes to whom we don't show God's love.

Personal Reflection: Make an effort to recognize that every person you see throughout this week is loved by God and try to demonstrate that love to them. Find a specific person that you want to out-love. Write about how it goes.

_____

_____

_____

_____

_____

WHO'S DRIVING?

*Jeremiah 29:11 – "'For I know the plans I have for you,'
declares the Lord, 'plans to prosper you and not to harm
you; plans to give you a hope and a future.'" (NIV)*

What does it mean to be a Christian? If someone were to ask you that, what would you answer?

Are you familiar with the board game Life? I used to *love* playing it with my dad. In that game, you have tiny cars with tiny "people" that you put inside, and that car represents your life journey. You move that car and the miniature version of you along the "path of life" (the spaces on the board), trying to reach the destination.

Imagine that you are driving through your life journey on the path of life. Many people think that becoming a Christian means that you stop your "car" long enough to let God get into the passenger seat beside you, and then you keep driving with Him sitting next to you.

You're taking God with you, which is good … but did

you notice who is still driving the car? You are. You're still making all the decisions, taking all the turns you want to, etc. God is just along for the ride.

But that's not what true Christianity looks like.

Truly being a Christian—truly having faith—means that we are called to surrender. That means we stop the car, get out, let God into the driver's seat of our lives, and then *we* sit in the passenger seat. We give God full control over our lives. Whatever He chooses to do, whichever road He takes us on, we trust in our Driver no matter what and in His plan more than ours.

If that seems scary to you, you're right. It is scary and hard. I struggle with it all the time. Please don't hear me telling you that I do this perfectly—I definitely don't. I always want to shout, "GOD, NOT *THAT* WAY!" or take the wheel back from Him and drive from the passenger side like in a scene from an action movie. I think I'm saving the day by taking back control, but I'm not. Most of the time, that's when the characters end up in epic crashes.

Am I taking this metaphor too far? Probably. Anyway ....

The point is, we are called to be *followers* of Christ, not *leaders* of Christ. That means He has to be the One in the lead! He knows this is hard for us. He doesn't call us to surrender because He's trying to hurt us, but because, as our verse says, He has a perfect plan for us. He will ultimately take us to a better destination than we ever could have planned for ourselves. He knows what He's doing.

If you've never done so, take a moment to get out of the driver's seat of your life today. Let God take over. Give Him the wheel, and then, no matter what comes next, trust in your Driver.

Personal Reflection: In what area(s) do you need to switch seats with God today? Write out a prayer below letting God know you want HIM to be the driver of your life.

_____

_____

_____

_____

_____

_____

_____

_____

_____

_____

_____

_____

_____

_____

REMEMBER

Psalm 77:11 - "I will remember the works of the Lord ..." (NKJV)

We've spent some time throughout this book comparing and contrasting two separate words. We'll do that a little more later, but today, we're just going to look at one word.

That word is *remember*. It means "to recall to the mind by an act or effort of memory."[8]

When you're in the middle of a bad situation, a crisis, or just a bad day, it's easy to lose sight of some very important truths that we all need to hold onto. In those moments, our minds often go to bad places, don't they? But what if we tried to set our minds on something better?

One reason I love the definition cited above is that it includes the word "effort." That shows me that choosing to change our thoughts is not immediate or

8. *Dictionary.com*, s.v. "remember," accessed August 3, 2025, https://www.dictionary.com/browse/remember

involuntary. Sometimes it's not at all easy, but if we choose what we remember in those moments, that effort could change everything.

So, by now you're probably asking, "What am I supposed to remember?" Here are three points that I want us to try to make an effort to recall in the middle of that tough time:

1. *Who and what God is.* Here are some examples, just to get you started: *God is in control. God is directing our story. God is good. God is with us.*

2. *What God has done.* We should always start by remembering what He did on the cross. At times, we all overlook that or forget its significance, but it should never be an afterthought. Also, we should remember what He's done in our personal journeys. How has God carried you through past trials or difficulties you didn't think you could get through? What did God teach you during those?

3. *Who you are to God.* You are loved by Him. Chosen by Him. Fought for by Him.

This always makes me think of the Israelites and the stories we find of them in the Bible. God did miracle after miracle to get the Israelites out of Egypt, but after a while, they started forgetting everything that God had done. He defeated Pharoah with the plagues. He parted the sea. He sent food from heaven.

But instead of thanking Him for those miracles and trusting Him with the next steps, they complained when met with challenges and said they couldn't go on. I'm so quick to judge them for that ... but don't I do the same? Don't you?

Next time you're going through a hard day, make an *effort* to *remember* who God is, what He has done, and who you are to Him.

Personal Reflection: What's the first thing that comes to your mind during a tough day? Could you make an effort to think of the three points listed above instead? Try it out and see ... how does it change your perspective, your attitude, your testimony/ witness to others?

_____

_____

_____

_____

_____

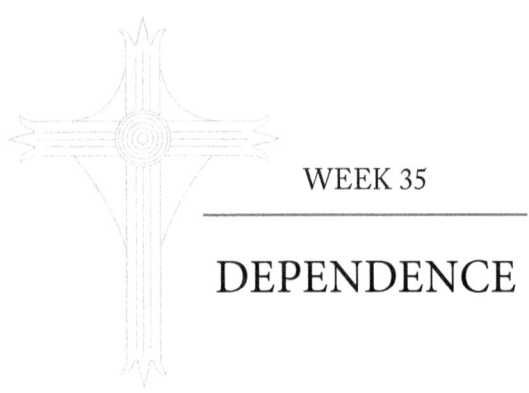

WEEK 35

DEPENDENCE

Psalm 23:1 - "The Lord is my shepherd, I lack nothing."
(NIV)

I heard someone say once that when we feel our life is uncertain or unknown, it's actually a good thing because that's the way it should be. My immediate response was, "I'm sorry, *what*? I don't think so!"

I know what uncertainty feels like. I know what it's like to look into the future and only see great big unknowns ahead. Personally, I don't care for it. I want to go back to the days when I knew what was going to happen next, when I wasn't constantly wondering what was going on, when things felt solid.

Can you relate to any of that? So, what on earth was that person talking about?!

I think what they meant was that it's during those times where we really understand and start to live out our dependence on God.

When we can't depend on circumstances ....

When we can't depend on our own abilities ....

When we can't depend on friends or family or the things that we always thought we could depend on ....

We can *always* depend on God. And it's when those other things are taken away, when life suddenly seems clouded by our circumstances, that we truly start depending on God alone.

Think about it this way. If you understood everything, then why would you need faith? If you knew where you were going, why would you need a Guide? If life weren't uncertain, would you ever truly learn that your only real certainty lies in God? When you don't know the answers, when you can't see the way forward, when you don't understand why, that's when you grow your dependence on Him.

And as Christians, isn't one of our main goals to grow our relationship with God and become more dependent on Him? That's where the statement comes: *When life is uncertain, that's the way it should be.*

Sometimes we get the opportunity to know what will happen; sometimes not. Sometimes we can see; sometimes we can't. But the definition of true dependence on Him is learning to be okay either way. It's not letting either scenario shake you because either way, you're standing firmly in God.

This is hard to accept. But look at Psalm 23:1. When you truly believe that God is your Shepherd and you depend on Him no matter what happens next, you lack *nothing*.

Personal Reflection: Read over Psalm 23 and write about how deep David's dependence on God is through this passage.

_____

_____

_____

_____

_____

_____

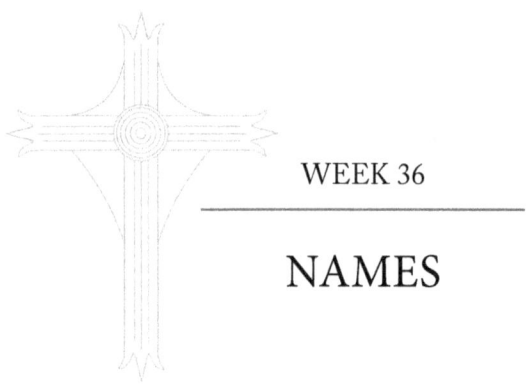

NAMES

Psalm 9:10 – "And those who know Your name will put their trust in You ..." (NKJV)

D o you know what your name means? My best friend reminds me all the time that my name, Jordan, means "descending." I was named after the Jordan River in the Bible, which *descends* into the Dead Sea. Many amazing things happened in the Bible regarding the Jordan River, including Jesus's baptism! What's the story behind your name?

Have you ever taken time to look at all the names God is called in the Bible? Have you ever looked to see what those names mean? Much like the names we each have (or maybe even more so in Biblical times), each name has a specific meaning and reasoning for it. God didn't put those names in the Bible to bulk up His reputation or give Himself more credentials. He put those names there because He knew that we would need each one of them in our lives.

Let's look at a few examples.

If you're feeling alone, remember He is EMMANUEL, which means "God with us" (Mt. 1:23)

If you're feeling afraid or anxious, remember He is the PRINCE OF PEACE. (Isa. 9:6)

If you're feeling invisible or unknown, remember He is the GOD WHO SEES. (Gen. 16:13)

If you're in need of provision, He is your PROVIDER (Gen. 22:14)

If you think you've made too many mistakes or gone too far, He is your REDEEMER (Ps. 78:35).

If you're feeling unloved, He is your ABBA ("Father") who loves you more than you can imagine. (Rom. 8:15).

Do you see how each one means something that speaks to a struggle or difficulty we might wrestle with? I love how God does this! He knows what we feel and what we're going through, and He has already shown that whatever we need, He provides. These are just a few examples—I encourage you to go through and find your own that speak to you. Look at all the names of God, and thank Him for what each one says about Him.

Personal Reflection: Which name of God listed here means the most to you and why? If you were to write out your own "Name of God" statement based on what you're feeling or going through, what would it be?

_____

_____

_____

_____

_____

_____

_____

_____

_____

_____

_____

_____

_____

IN THE MOMENT

Psalm 118:24 - "This is the day the Lord has made; we will rejoice and be glad in it." (NKJV)

I was in a small group once where, at the very end of the meeting, we all went around and gave our prayer requests. One girl's prayer request struck me. She asked for prayer that she could stay present in the moment.

At first, I thought that was a strange request. Others were praying for health or upcoming exams or other specific concerns that were on their hearts ... and then there was her desire to be present. However, as I went on throughout the following weeks, months, and even years, her prayer request kept coming back into my mind, and I started to see the value of it.

How often do you struggle with being present? If you're having trouble answering, let me ask it differently: how often do you find yourself worrying about future events? Now, how often do you find yourself replaying the past? Does that help put things into perspective a little bit more?

I know it did for me because my answer to both those questions would be ALL. THE. TIME.

Whether I'm worrying about the future or obsessing over the past, I am always doing one or the other. If there are things in my future that I'm concerned about, worry will take all my focus and time. I will go over every possible worst-case scenario in my head.

But if there's not some big, scary thing up ahead of me, then my mind automatically starts going back over old memories! Maybe it's an old crisis that I didn't handle well, or maybe it's just an old conversation I'll replay in my head, thinking of all the things I should have said differently.

What is the problem with living this way? Well, I can think of a few:

We can't control the future ... or change the past. Worrying won't do anything to prevent the future events we are so concerned about. And that past we keep replaying? We can't change anything that happened.

We're missing the present moment. While we're fixated on other things, the current moment is passing us by. It's a gift from God, a blessing that we can't get back. And by missing that ...

... we're missing what God wants for us and where God meets us. He is outside of time. He isn't bound by moments like we are. He created time that way for us for a reason. He knows what we can and can't handle, and He meets us in

the present moment—which is just where He wants us to be.

You might be thinking, what if the present moment is bad? What if the only way you get through the present moment is by taking your mind off it? Let me encourage you by saying again that *the present moment is where God meets you.* He gives you strength enough for each present moment. He gives grace for each present moment.

Life is filled with millions of moments, and no matter what they contain, whether we see them as good or bad, each is a gift. Let's all try to be present in the moment we have right now.

Personal Reflection: Go through this week trying to be present in each moment, good or bad, and trust that God will meet you there.

_____

_____

_____

_____

BURIED BLESSINGS

James 1:17 - "Every good and perfect gift is from above ..." (NIV)

Several weeks ago, we talked about the importance of counting our blessings ... how this practice reminds us of God's faithfulness and uplifts us. But what about the times when even getting started with counting our blessings feels like a struggle?

I think we can all agree that sometimes, finding blessings takes a little more work than others. There are those incredible moments where we're watching a gorgeous sunset or surrounded by loved ones that we can't help but feel blessed. But what about all the other times? What about the hard days, weeks, months when it feels like you're barely getting by?

That's when it's time for you to look for *buried blessings*.

This is an idea that has helped me personally through many difficult times, and I've even passed it onto friends as well.

I could go with a couple different analogies to describe buried blessings, and I've been debating which one I want to use. You're probably thinking after seeing the word "buried" that I'm going to relate it to searching for treasure amongst the dirt or digging up archaeological finds. While those are good, there's an analogy that fits even better.

I saw an experiment once where people were shown a simple white screen. There was nothing special on it at all—just a blank page. Then, they were given special glasses. Once they had these glasses on, their entire view changed. That boring, plain white screen suddenly turned into a beautiful picture filled with color! The lens in the glasses changed everything and allowed them to see beauty they didn't even know was there!

That is the idea I want you to get here. So many of us go through our days just looking at the "colorless" parts of our lives without realizing what we are missing. I have seen firsthand that God gives us these buried blessings all the time—especially when we are hurting the most. When we start learning to look for them, it becomes easier to see our hard circumstances from God's perspective.

That's why this is my favorite analogy. Learn to put on the right "lens," if you will, and you will learn to let those blessings bring color into your days.

I don't know the exact details of what this will look like for you. Maybe it's a small thing that works out when you didn't expect it to. Maybe it's a phone call or text when you need it. Maybe it's a song that comes on the radio that speaks to you. You get the idea.

When I think of buried blessings, I think of my dad. He looks for them all the time, and it inspires me. One time, after a crazy couple of days when things were really tough, my dad simply smiled in the midst of the chaos around me and said "Look how beautiful the blue sky is today!" I looked at him and thought, *Wow, I want to do that!*

These little blessings are actually big. They remind us that God is with us and that God sees exactly where we are and exactly what we're struggling with. Look for these small blessings; let them take your plain, boring, or even downright dark days and turn them into something beautiful.

Personal Reflection: Take this next week and begin looking for "buried blessings" everywhere. How many did you find?

_____

_____

_____

_____

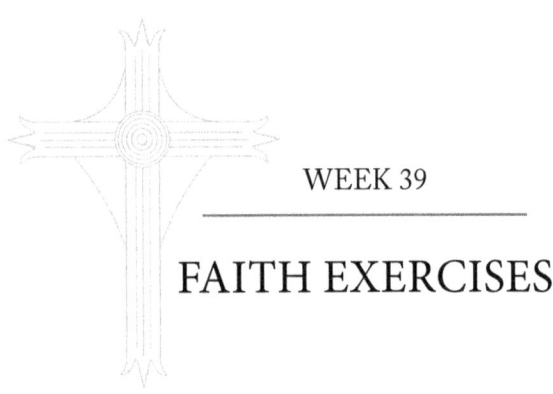

FAITH EXERCISES

2 Peter 3:18 – "But grow in the grace and knowledge of our Lord and Savior Jesus Christ ..." (NKJV)

My mom has taught aerobics for over thirty years. Ever since COVID hit, she has taught her classes virtually from our home, which means that I now have the chance to participate in them!

When I say "participate," I mean stand behind the camera and operate the technical side. I'm mostly behind the scenes, but for just a few minutes during every class, she will call me in front of the camera, right beside her, and we will do an exercise together. Something that I've noticed about those exercises is that they're *hard*. I only do three minutes of an hour-long class, and that is enough for me!

I once heard someone refer to the Christian walk of faith as an "exercise." This person called faith a "muscle" that must be strengthened, and because of helping my mom, you can imagine how that stuck with me. I know a few things about exercises because of her (I should probably dedicate this devotional to her!), so here are some things that stand out to me about that analogy.

As I've already covered, exercises are hard. They're also pretty painful at times. They're not meant to be easy; my mom always says that easy exercises don't do any good. In the same way, it's okay to admit that when our faith is "exercised," it's really hard. It's painful. We won't enjoy it.

Another important thing is that the instructor matters. (I guarantee you, this will be my mom's favorite part!) You have to completely trust your instructor while taking exercise classes and you have to believe that they are taking you through that pain for a reason. Most importantly, you have to follow what they tell you to do.

Our Instructor (God) knows what's best for us. If He's leading us through faith exercises that are difficult, we have to follow Him and trust that He's doing it for a reason. A good instructor doesn't just tell you what to do and stand there—they go through the pain with you. God instructs us, but also walks beside us each step of our journey, guiding us through it all. Hebrews 4:15 even tells us that He empathizes with us and feels everything that we feel.

In the end, you'll find that physical exercises have made you stronger. You don't see it right away. It takes time. But eventually, you see that your body reaped the benefits of the pain and effort of working those muscles. When we go through "faith exercises," we are being given opportunities to grow in our faith, in our strength, and ultimately in our *knowledge of Christ!*

As hard as they are, we'll look back one day and see how all of the exercises were designed just for us by an Instructor who knew exactly what He was doing.

Personal Reflection: Is God giving you "faith exercises" right now? What is your Instructor saying? Which faith muscles are you strengthening?

_____

_____

_____

_____

_____

_____

_____

_____

_____

_____

_____

_____

_____

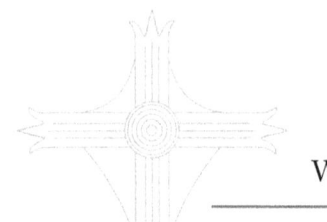

THROUGH GOD'S EYES

1 Samuel 16:7 - "... For the Lord does not see as man sees ..." (NKJV)

A professor in my online theology class once asked us what the top three most important things in our lives were. It didn't take too long for me to come up with what my answer would be: 1. God, 2. family, and 3. friends. *mic drop!*

That's the perfect answer, right? I was totally positive that I had come up with the most Christian, most appropriate, all-around best answer possible. Check that off the list, moving on. Now I just hope that's on the test so I can get an A+!

But then, the professor said something that burst my bubble pretty quickly: having God on your list is the wrong answer.

How can that be?! I thought. *What am I possibly missing here?* Yet, my professor's explanation has always stuck with me. While putting God as number one on our list is a good thing, we should put Him first in *every area of our lives.*

The idea here is to go deeper, to go beyond the earthly priorities we can come up with. Why? Because God being number one on our list still puts God *on a list.* It puts Him on a list that I am in charge of creating; therefore, I become the one who decides His worth and His value. I essentially rank Him. Even if I say He has a higher value to me than other things, that still centers totally on me.

I make the decision. That still gives *me* the power to put God where *I* want Him to be. In doing this, I am making myself bigger than God, and my thoughts thus become more valuable than God's. Do you see how this is a different perspective?

Needless to say, by the end of the class lecture, I was glad that question was *not* on the test! But it got me thinking … what would life look like if we tried to see everything through God's eyes? If I can be so sure that I got the perfect answer and still miss it by so much, what other areas of my perspective need shifting?

I won't lie. I am sure there are other areas where I am making it all about me when it should be all about Him. If I tried to change this, what would happen? Would I be grieved by the same things that grieve Him? Excited by the things that make Him happy? Would my view of people or even myself change?

So, here's my proposal: for this upcoming week, let's try

this out. Let's make our prayer for this week something like the following:

Lord, let me see everything in my life—the good, the bad, the in-between—through Your eyes today.

It might just change the way we see everything.

Personal Reflection: Try doing this throughout the week and write about your experiences. What did it change for you? How?

_____

_____

_____

_____

_____

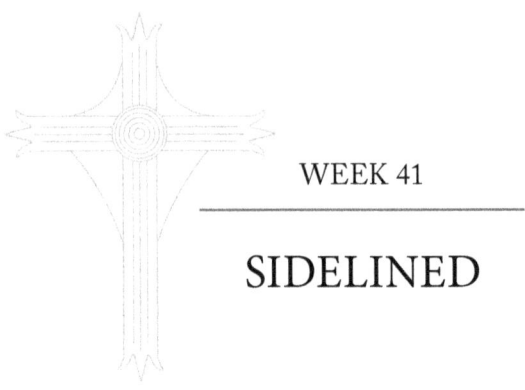

SIDELINED

Psalm 4:3 - "Know that the Lord has set apart His faithful servant for Himself; the Lord hears when I call to Him." (NIV)

Do you like watching sports? I definitely do—I am a *diehard* Pittsburgh Steelers and Atlanta Braves fan! That scream that you heard on November 2, 2021, when the Braves won the World Series? Yeah, that was me. I was so excited. I'm still waiting on the Steelers to give me a Super Bowl win (that I'm old enough to understand watching).

As much as I love watching sports, though, there is something that I don't think any sports-lover enjoys: seeing players get sidelined. And if we hate watching it, imagine how the players feel! They've got to be watching all the star players in action and wishing they were part of it. Maybe they're even imagining what they would do if they were back out there on the field. Meanwhile, all they can do is sit on the sidelines.

Have you ever felt like *you* were being sidelined in life? Like you were suddenly taken off the field you wanted to play on, out of the spotlight, away from all you've dreamed of, and forced to just sit and watch?

My lung transplant sidelines me all the time, and therefore, it sidelines my whole family. There are countless examples of in-person events my family and I can't attend because I can't be exposed to people. It can be so hard to understand why things like that happen and pretty much impossible to accept them.

But look at verses like Romans 8:28 or Jeremiah 29:11 (which we already talked about in devotionals 13 and 33). Do we really believe those are true? If we do, what do we make of these sidelining struggles? How can they be used for good? How can God still have a perfect plan for us? How do we go about believing those beautiful promises amidst the painful realities we face?

I have two responses to that. First, we aren't sidelined by accident. Even if it seems like a surprise or a disaster to us, God knew it was coming, and in His wisdom, He will use it for good.

I know it doesn't seem like it at the time, but your suffering has a purpose. Maybe, if it's temporary, it's a time where He's calling you to just rest and focus on Him, or maybe He's preparing you for something more to come. Or, if it seems permanent, maybe He's showing you that the sidelines are where He wants you to be, even if it's hard to understand why.

I'll leave you with this different way to think of it: are you being sidelined, or are you being *set apart* by God? The world will tell you the sidelines are a bad place to be and that nothing good can come from it. But God has a special plan just for you, and if that's where God's calling you to be, is there a better place?

Personal Reflection: Are you "sidelined" now? How so? What ways might God be using this situation in your life?

_____

_____

_____

_____

_____

_____

_____

LOVE

1 Corinthians 16:14 - "Do everything in love." (NIV)

We've talked about the importance of words throughout this book. Now, let's take that idea in a bit of a different direction. We all know those very common "Christian" words that you frequently hear in Christian circles. But do we really understand what they mean or what God wants us to do with them?

For these next four devotionals, we're going to look at four separate "Christian" words: love, hope, grace, and joy. Today, we're going to focus on love, which has deep biblical meaning for how Jesus wants us to treat one another.

When thinking of "love," my mind immediately goes to 1 Corinthians 13, which lays out what love looks like. This is the kind of love that Jesus calls us to embrace. As you read the following passage, ask yourself, "How many of these traits do I embody?" No one will do all of them—or any of them—perfectly, but reading through these verses can help us see some areas that we maybe need to work on. How many of these aspects of love can be said of you?

1 Corinthians 13:4-7 - "Love is patient, love is kind. It does not envy, it does not boast, it is not proud. It does not dishonor others, it is not self-seeking, it is not easily angered, it keeps no record of wrongs. Love does not delight in evil but rejoices with the truth. It always protects, always trusts, always hopes, always perseveres."

That presents a lot to work on, doesn't it? I know it certainly does for me! If reading this verse and considering how you measure up leaves you feeling discouraged, don't worry—I want to end on something that should be a comfort and an encouragement to all of us.

1 John 4:19 gives us the reason why we want to love: "We love because He first loved us." We love others because we have seen and experienced the incredible love that God shows each of us.

Now, re-read the passage above, but with a different mindset this time. Read it and realize that God is the only One who does each and every one of these things *perfectly*. He embodies each one of these beautiful traits perfectly. He loves perfectly.

Personal Reflection: Which one of these love traits do you need to focus on a little more? Who can you show more love to this week?

_____

_____

_____

_____

_____

_____

_____

_____

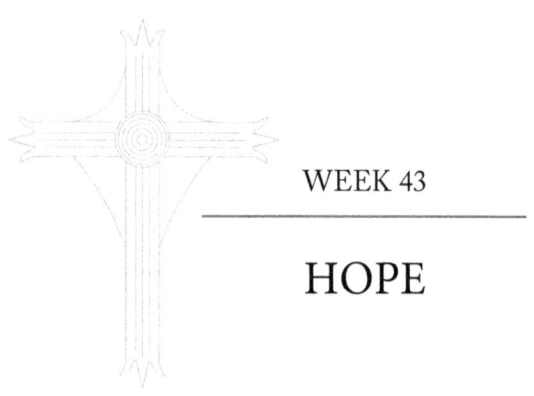

WEEK 43

HOPE

Lamentations 3:24 - "'The Lord is my portion,' says my soul, 'Therefore I hope in Him!'" (NKJV)

What is this idea of having *hope?* Perhaps more importantly, how do we go about actually having it? Is it something that's even attainable in this fallen, difficult, disappointing world?

The Bible talks often about hope, including in the verse above, which says that we are to hope *in* something, or rather in someone: the Lord. How does being a Christian give us the ability to hope in the Lord in the midst of everything we still have to deal with?

We've already talked before about how I've suffered from migraines ever since I was young. The only real fix for them is to take strong migraine medication and wait for it to take effect. During those hours I've spent in bed with a cold compress over my eyes, I've had lots of time to think! It occurred to me once how big a difference it makes to me whether or not I've already taken the migraine medication—not just physically, but mentally. I would still be in the same amount of pain, struggling in the same dark room, but knowing I had taken the medication helped me handle it all so much better somehow.

Then, it hit me: That difference is hope. What changed was that I now had the knowledge that soon I would get better. I had *hope* that the medicine would do its job and I'd be back on my feet in a little while. I could look forward with the expectation that things would improve.

There's a big difference between believing the healing is coming, that things will get better and you only have to hold on, and feeling the despair of thinking that healing isn't coming and that the struggle is all you'll ever feel. That is what hope is.

As Christians, our hope comes from something so much more reliable than migraine meds—it comes from Jesus! That's what it means to put our hope in Him. It means that we can look to Him and all that He has done for us, knowing that He has promised that someday, whether in this life or beyond, things will get better.

It doesn't mean we won't feel the pain. Those who have hope aren't immune to feeling the hurt that this world brings to all of us. But it does mean we know a Healer who will eventually make all things perfect, beautiful, and whole again. Maybe we won't see it in this lifetime, but we can know it will happen.

Being a Christian doesn't take us out of the pain, but gives us a constant reason to hope in the midst of the pain: that one day, God will make all things new. No matter what your circumstances are, that is how you can hope in the Lord!

Personal Reflection: Do you need to hear this message of hope? What does the idea of hope in the Lord change for you?

_____

_____

_____

_____

_____

_____

_____

_____

_____

_____

_____

_____

_____

WEEK 44

GRACE

Ephesians 2:8 - "For it is by grace you have been saved, through faith—and this is not from yourselves, it is the gift of God." (NIV)

I won't lie—this devotional is very tricky for me to write. The concept of *grace* is one that I struggle to wrap my mind around, but I think if we dive into it together, looking at a few different sides of God's grace, we'll find ourselves so grateful that we did—and so grateful *for* that grace!

You've probably heard the term *grace* used most often the way it is in the verse above, one that you're likely familiar with if you're a Christian. This is where we'll start, because I don't ever want to overlook the amazing, life-changing grace that saves us. When we choose to trust in God and become a Christian, it is God's *grace* that allows us to be saved, to spend eternity with Him. We can do absolutely nothing to earn being saved by God; those who tell you that you can do enough good works or help enough people to merit being saved aren't recognizing this idea of grace.

This is exactly what the above verse is trying to warn us against. I've heard grace defined by some as *getting what we don't deserve*. If that idea doesn't sound quite right to you, it's probably because we all have such a warped idea of what exactly it is that we *do* deserve.

We've all sinned and fallen short of the glory of God (Rom. 3:23). What we *deserve* from God is permanent separation from Him, physical death, and eternal death in hell.

At some point, all of us have said the phrase, *"It's not fair!"* I was asked once by a teacher many, many years ago if I thought God was fair. "Of course," I replied. "How could He not be?"

Turns out I was wrong. God's not fair. He gives us so far above and beyond what fair would be. Praise God that He's not fair!

Still, most people stop at the idea of the grace that saves us. But there's more to grace than that. There is also the grace that *keeps* us—that constantly surrounds us, covers us, and keeps us going. I love how grace is described in our verse as *"the gift of God."* I can think of no better way to say it! It isn't just about our salvation; it's also every other gift. A warm bed at night, family, friends, sunsets—they're all gifts of grace from God.

Grace is the "safety net" that catches us when we fall, when we ultimately continue to mess up despite our best efforts.

Now, I want to be careful here. This is NOT me telling you that you can just go on and do whatever you want because of that grace. Instead, remember that it's a gift. We need to handle it well. Romans 6:1-2 reminds us that we cannot abuse God's grace by using it as a license to sin.

God's incredible gift of grace that saves us and keeps us is available to anyone who is willing to receive it, and that truly is *amazing grace*!

Personal Reflection: Did this devotional change your view of grace? How?

_____

_____

_____

_____

_____

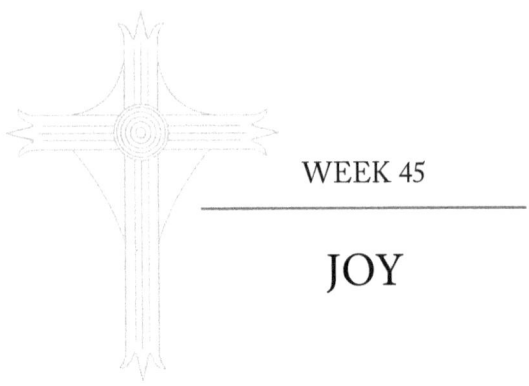

JOY

John 15:11 - "These things I have spoken to you, that My joy may remain in you, and that your joy may be full." (NKJV)

We're almost done with our mini-series on Christian words. The last one we will look at here is *joy*. But it's also a word-comparison devotional too—a two-for-one!

I say that because it's really easy for us to confuse *joy* with *happiness*, but there is a big difference, and that difference is what makes joy so beautiful. It all lies in what they are both rooted in.

Here's what I mean. Happiness is rooted in experiences and events that make us feel good. For instance, when the Steelers win, I am very happy. But the problem with that is it's a temporary feeling. Within a few days, the Steelers victory is not still making me happy, and within a few more days, they'll play again and potentially lose ... which definitely doesn't make me happy.

However, joy is deeper. Joy goes beyond circumstances—it is rooted in Christ. Christ is unchangeable (Heb 13:8); therefore, our joy is unchangeable. Because God is always with us, joy can always be with us too. In fact, I'm going to challenge us to find joy even in the places where it seems the least likely to be found.

Here is a simple little exercise you can do to demonstrate what I mean. Grab a pen and write down the least joyful thing you experience. What is the thing (or things) that steals your joy the most? Got it?

Okay ... now, search the Scriptures and write down a promise of God that speaks to that situation. Here are a few of mine so you can see what I'm talking about:

When life feels out of control ...
I know God is in control (Isa. 14:24).

When the storms of life are raging ...
I know God is in them with me (Josh. 1:9).

When my health and my life are uncertain ...
I know God is constant (Mal. 3:6).

Do you see how remembering these truths about God can bring joy into these circumstances? Even though they are *hard,* real, and painful, there is still joy to be found in them when we are rooted in Jesus.

Personal Reflection: Write down your joy-sentence(s) here.

_____

_____

_____

_____

_____

_____

_____

STRENGTH IN WEAKNESS

2 Corinthians 12:10 – "That is why, for Christ's sake, I delight in weaknesses ... For when I am weak, then I am strong." (NIV)

Do you view yourself as a strong person? If you said no, then ... first of all, same! But second, this devotional is for you.

If you said yes, then congrats. I think it's awesome that you can say that but, read through this devotional anyway. James 1:2 says that we must "count it all joy *when* we fall into various trials"—not "if." This makes it clear that there will come a future time when circumstances seem to strip you of that strength.

The topic of strength has always been important to me personally. I can't explain why, but I have always had this need for others to see me as a strong person. I have incredible friends who have called me strong before, and that is one of the biggest compliments they could give me. It will mean the world to me and stick with me for a long time. I sometimes wonder if the reason for this is that I feel so much like the opposite, as if the less strong I *feel*, the stronger I need to *portray* that I am.

However, when I do that, I am going about the goal of finding strength in the wrong way.

The world wants us to focus on our own strength. We need to "find our inner strength" because it's there deep inside us. We are strong enough to handle anything—we just need to dig deep and tap into that strength.

However, as He does with all things the world teaches, God says the opposite. God says that we aren't the source of strength at all. We're humans, and we don't have limitless strength to tap into.

But do you know who does? God!

Every year, I used to start out trying different resolutions like "have courage," "be a conqueror," etc. Within a week, I gave up on it in frustration. I finally figured out why: those goals all focused on me being my own source of strength. That's not what God designed me for. *He* is the source of all strength.

So now, I choose new year's goals such as "trust more," "have faith over fear," etc.—goals that re-center myself on God's strength, not my own. We as humans are weak, but God doesn't hate us for that weakness. Instead, Psalm 86:15 tells us our God is a "compassionate and gracious God" (NIV). He has compassion and love for us and chooses to give us His strength. *That* is how we can say that we are strong even in our weaknesses, like the verse above says: because we don't live through our strength, but through His.

Personal Reflection: How can you rely on His strength instead of your own?

_____

_____

_____

_____

_____

_____

_____

_____

_____

_____

_____

_____

_____

_____

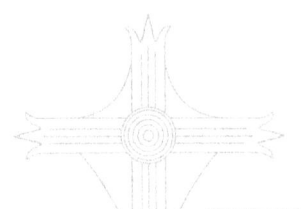

ACHIEVER VS. BELIEVER

Romans 10:11 - "... anyone who believes in Him will never be put to shame." (NIV)

A s we go through this word-comparison devotional, I want you to be thinking of the following questions. First, do you put more effort into being an achiever or a believer? Second, would you rather be described as an achiever or a believer?

As we always do, we'll start out with the definitions of each word. Here's the thing, though ... I don't love the actual definitions of these two words. While accurate, they don't get at the point I'm trying to make. So, instead of giving you the official definitions like I normally do, I'm giving you *my* definitions of them.

Achiever: Someone who focuses on worldly success; who seeks to make their name great.

Believer: Someone who focuses on eternal success; who seeks to make God's name great above his/her own.

Now, I want to start out by being clear about something. Unlike the other words we've covered where God specifically calls us *not* to do one of the two, being an achiever is not a bad thing! It is great to work hard and strive to achieve great accomplishments. In fact, God calls us to do everything we do as if we're working unto Him (Col. 3:23), and He may very well bless you with achievements.

But the idea here is this: which one is more important to you? I ask you this question because the world asks it all the time in different ways. The world will make us choose which one means more to us. Sometimes, we'll be asked to compromise our faith in order to get that big promotion or that dream job. We need to have our answers ready when those moments come. Which title would you rather have: achiever or believer?

I think it's clear which one God is calling us to have in those moments: that of believer. Ultimately, when our lives end, that is the only title that will matter at all. What job position you held, how many people knew your name, how much money you made, whether you were in charge or not ... none of that will matter. Believing in Jesus Christ, accepting Him as your Savior, and all that you choose to do for His glory—that's all that will matter.

I hope by now that we are all willing to stand firm, no matter what happens, as unwavering *believers*.

Personal Reflection: Look at your own life ... are there areas where you are choosing between the road of a believer and the road of an achiever? Which are you choosing and, based on that answer, what needs to change?

_____

_____

_____

_____

_____

_____

_____

_____

_____

_____

_____

_____

_____

_____

_____

VICTORY

Deuteronomy 20:4 - "For the Lord your God is the one who goes with you to fight for you against your enemies to give you victory." (NIV)

Do you ever struggle with feeling defeated? Maybe you turn on the news and see all the wars, political turmoil, natural disasters, etc., or maybe you fight your own wars and have your own inner turmoil that no one ever sees. It might not be on the news for all to watch, but it's very real in your life.

The Bible makes it clear that we will fight spiritual battles throughout our faith journey as well, but does it ever seem like those are too hard to win? If you can relate to this, I want our verse to encourage you today. Let's take a moment to meditate on each piece of it.

First, we see that *God goes with us.* We're never in battle alone. He says this multiple times in Scripture, including in my favorite verse, Joshua 1:9, which we talked about earlier. The Lord is always with us. He doesn't ever let us go or leave our side. This is a beautiful promise that we never should overlook or take for granted.

But it goes beyond that. It also says that *God fights for us*. Notice that God doesn't say "I'll go with you but I'll stay a safe distance away," or "I'll come but just to watch and see what happens." He chooses to fight our battles for us! Exodus 14:14 echoes this same amazing promise when it says, "The Lord will fight for you; you need only to be still."

Pause for a second with that idea. The God of the universe not only knows your name, not only chooses to be with you, but also chooses to step into your battles and fight for you. Wow! He is always fighting for us, even when we can't see it. As Romans 8:31 says, "If God is for us, who can be against us?"

Finally, He fights *to give us the victory*. Think about the certainty in that statement. It doesn't say, "Hopefully we'll come out with a victory," or, "We'll try our best and see what we can do." No—when He is fighting for us, we can *know* we have the ultimate victory! Maybe not the victory that we were thinking of or hoping for here on this earth, but ultimately, we can know that death, Satan, pain, and darkness are all defeated for good in Heaven.

We're on the winning side. There's no uncertainty there. The victory is His. Always.

Be encouraged by this today. God is with us. He fights for us. He always gets the victory!

Personal Reflection: Write down some of the battles you are facing. How does this verse meet you in the middle of those and encourage you?

_____

_____

_____

_____

_____

_____

_____

THE REAL DEAL

Psalm 119:160 - "The entirety of Your word is truth ..." (NKJV)

Have you ever struggled to know what the truth is? Have you ever believed a lie? There are SO many voices claiming to have their own "truths" about how we should view the world. How can we be sure of which one is actually true? Maybe it's a lie you believe about yourself— voices in your head that you've heard so many times that you've just accepted them. Is there even a way to decipher the voice of God versus the voice of lies?

If you're struggling with discerning truth from lies, this analogy may help. There are people in the FBI who are specifically trained to recognize whether money is counterfeit or not. If you were in that position, how would you try to tell if a dollar bill is a legitimate piece of money or if it's fake? When I heard this story for the first time, I thought immediately that I'd take time to study the fake one. What does it look like? How does it differ from the real thing?

But that's not how they do it. Instead, they choose to study the real dollar. I mean, really, seriously study the real one to the point where they know every detail about it—its color, texture, weight, etc. When they know what the real one looks like, the fake one is easy to spot.

Let's say I offered to pay you twenty dollars, and I gave you the choice between a real twenty-dollar bill and a piece of paper that I just wrote a great big "20" on. Of course, you would pick the real one. But how would you know that? You've never seen my drawing before; you didn't have time to study it. What would make you so sure that the twenty-dollar bill I was offering was real and the paper drawing was fake? Because you have seen what a real twenty-dollar bill looks like so often that you would easily tell mine was wrong. *Because you know the real deal.*

The voice of Truth is God's Word—the Real Deal.

But then the question becomes, do we know the Bible well enough? Have we studied it so much that when counterfeits come and claim to be real, we can easily see right through them? Those lies that we believe—can learning what the Real Deal has to say change our views on them? On the world? On ourselves? I believe it can!

God gave us His Word for this purpose: so that we could know Him and learn to live by what He says. He knows there are constant voices that try to pull us away with the lies they tell, and He knows they each claim to be the "truth." But He gave us a weapon against those false voices: His Word. Jesus Himself used this weapon to combat Satan's lies when He was tempted in Matthew 4. Each of the three times Satan comes to Jesus with a new temptation, we see the same response from Jesus: quoting God's Word. If we will take the time to study it, hear what He says to us, and understand what the real Truth is, then we will be able to say for certain that we know the Real Deal.

Personal Reflection: What lies do you struggle with believing when you shouldn't? What does the Real Deal have to say about them?

_____

_____

_____

_____

_____

_____

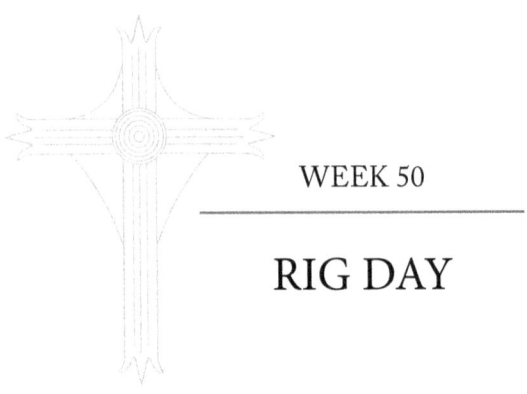

WEEK 50

BIG DAY

Matthew 11:28 - "Come to Me, all you who are weary and burdened, and I will give you rest." (NIV)

If you started this weekly devotional book in January, then you're probably in the full swing of the Christmas season right now. This is my absolute favorite time of the year, but like every season, it can have its challenges.

During the month of December and the Christmas season, does life often just feel like a juggling act? Like all you're doing is focusing on keeping all the balls you're "juggling" in the air? We have some actual juggling balls in our house, and I like to juggle them sometimes. The most I can juggle is three at a time, and sometimes that doesn't even go as planned.

But in life, it can often feel like we're "juggling" an infinite number—especially at Christmas. We've got special meals to prepare, presents to buy, Christmas cards to mail, decorations to put up, etc. If you've got tough family

202

situations or complicated medical conditions, you're just adding many more balls into the mix.

Here's something I've noticed while trying to get better with those actual juggling balls: juggling takes all your focus. You can't look at anything else, or you'll end up dropping the balls. That's no big deal when it's me in my living room just playing around, but in the analogy of "juggling" real-life issues, that's stressful! It's anxiety-provoking. It takes the joy away from your days.

More than anything else, it takes our focus away from the reason for the season: *Jesus.*

I'm using Christmas as an example because that's where you probably are right now, but this isn't just a Christmastime issue. We are always "juggling" schedules or plans or worries—you name what it is for you right now.

I want to share something my mom came up with to help me during the worst stretch of time I had ever experienced. I was struggling in a way I never had before, and each day held at least one complete breakdown because of how overwhelmed by my situation I felt. Harping on that situation constantly kept me in a bad place. So, my mom came up with a RIG day.

"What exactly are we rigging?" you may ask. But in this case, it's an acronym. RIG means **R**est **I**n **G**od. For one day a week, (I think it was Wednesdays if I remember right) I wouldn't allow myself to worry about that situation at all. I'd just try to rest in the knowledge of who God is. It helped.

Do you need a RIG day in your life right now? Maybe you need to make this Christmas season a RIG season where you spend time just resting and reflecting on what the season really is.

I'm not telling you that your priorities aren't important or to completely forget about them. Things need done. Tasks need addressing. I would never ask you to throw up your hands and pretend it all didn't exist. During my RIG days, I didn't just stay in bed all day and deny my problems. Instead, I'm asking that, in whatever we are doing, we take the time to let our minds and hearts Rest In God.

Listen to Christian music. Repeat a Bible verse over to yourself. You will never regret the time you choose to spend putting down the "juggling balls," just for a little while, and Resting In God.

Personal Reflection: Pick a RIG day or a RIG season for your life and write about how it goes. Did that time help you? How?

_____

_____

_____

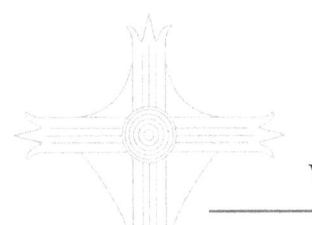

THE BEAUTIFUL-BROKEN

Ecclesiastes 3:11 - "He has made everything beautiful in its time ..." (NIV)

Does that title strike you as an oxymoron? I mean, how can something be broken and yet still be considered beautiful? Don't those two words seem to contradict each other so extremely that they just can't go together?

I have a small drawer in my bedroom armoire that I designated many years ago as a drawer for "special things." It was meant for those things that didn't really have any other place to go, but that I couldn't lose. I went through that drawer recently and was reminded of something: I broke quite a few things as a kid! That drawer held evidence of that; I found beads from an old necklace that I used to love and beads from ... well, I can't tell if it was a ring or a bracelet, honestly. I think it was a ring. But you get the point. The drawer contained lots of broken pieces of things that once were intact (oops!).

So, why would I keep these now broken pieces? Because to

me they're still beautiful. To me they still have value. I still love them, and since they're mine, I decide their value. And I say they're the beautiful-broken.

How broken do you think that you are? Maybe just a little cracked? Or maybe, you see yourself like those unrecognizable pieces in my drawer—broken beyond repair. But the great news is that you don't decide your value. You belong to God. You are His. Therefore, He decides what you are. And He says you are beautiful and priceless. He doesn't ignore your broken parts or try to cover them up. Instead, He meets you in them and still, even knowing every part of you, calls you His beautiful and precious child.

Many people think that, when we come to Him, we must do it "perfectly." We must fix ourselves or put ourselves together enough that we aren't broken before Him. We must put on the right face. But God says to come to Him, no matter what. He wants us to come to Him in that broken state to find our help in Him. He doesn't want our best side. He just wants our honest and broken prayers lifted up to Him because that's what He finds most beautiful.

Consider a mosaic. It's a beautiful work of art, right? When we look closely at it, though, we see that it's made up of pieces. To me, it almost looks like it's broken, but that's actually what makes it so cool. Even cooler than that is that it's the "broken pieces" aspect of it that makes the light shine through it. So, like that mosaic, let's try to view our broken pieces as the beautiful-broken; they can allow the Light of the One who's inside us to shine through even more!

Personal Reflection: Lift up your honest, broken prayers to God right now. Tell Him everything; don't try to sugarcoat or hide anything. You can even write a prayer here if you like. Know that God meets you there with so much love and compassion.

_____

_____

_____

_____

_____

_____

_____

_____

_____

_____

_____

_____

_____

_____

_____

ALWAYS

Matthew 28:20 - "… and surely I am with you always, to the very end of the age." (NIV)

Congratulations! We have officially reached the end of our journey together. Wow! I can't thank you enough—it's been an honor to walk with you through this past year. I'm praying this book has encouraged and uplifted you and shown you ways that you can choose to *Just Follow Jesus* in your life.

At the time I first began this book, I knew this was the devotional I wanted to end on because it's the message that I want to leave with you. You're about to enter into a new year, and I don't know what it will hold for you. But I know Who holds it. I know Who holds you through it.

It will probably be full of both good and bad moments, as with all of life. There will be times when your prayers are full of joy and thanks and praise and other times when they've turned to cries full of hurt and questions.

This poem was written from a stretch of time when it was the latter for me. I was wondering how God would respond to seeing me in uncertainty and pain. Then it hit me: He'd respond the same way He responds to every type of prayer, in every situation we face. No matter what happens in our lives, He will never change.

He's *always* on His throne. *Always* in control. *Always* holding us and *always* loving us. He is God. He is our Father. He is our Healer. He is our Savior. *Always.*

I've noticed that your prayers to Me
Have changed from what they used to be
They once were prayers of trust and praise
You felt so close to Me those days
But now I see tears fill your eyes
Your songs to Me have turned to cries
No longer do I hear you say
You trust that I will guide your way
And now you ask if I am there
Or if I even hear your prayer
Do I have a plan for you
And will I truly see you through
It breaks my heart each time I hear
You crying all those silent tears
Oh, how I wish that you could see
Just how much you mean to Me!
Though so, so much has changed for you
Nothing about Me is new
I'm in control, still on My throne
I'm holding you; you're not alone.

I am still worthy of your praise
I still love you and will ***always***.

God is good ... all the time!

Personal Reflection: How will you take what you've learned throughout this book with you stepping into the future? What do you feel as you look into this new year knowing God is with you always?

———————————————————————

———————————————————————

———————————————————————

———————————————————————

———————————————————————

_____

_____

_____

_____

_____

_____

_____

_____